THE PRESIDENTIAL DILEMMA

★★

THE PRESIDENTIAL DILEMMA
LEADERSHIP IN THE AMERICAN SYSTEM

Michael A. Genovese
Loyola Marymount University

■ HarperCollins*CollegePublishers*

Acquisitions Editor: Leo Wiegman
Project Editor: Marina Vaynshteyn
Art Director: Mary McDonnell
Text Designer: LaToya Wigfall
Cover Designer: John Sparks
Manufacturing Administrator: Alexandra Odulak
Desktop Administrator: LaToya Wigfall
Electronic Page Makeup: LaToya Wigfall
Printer and Binder: RR Donnelley & Sons Company
Cover Printer: RR Donnelley & Sons Company

THE PRESIDENTIAL DILEMMA: LEADERSHIP IN THE AMERICAN SYSTEM

Library of Congress Cataloging-in-Publication Data

Genovese, Michael A.
    The presidential dilemma : leadership in the American system /
Michael A. Genovese.
      p.   cm.
    Includes bibliographical references (p.   ) and index.
    ISBN 0-673-99278-0
    1. Presidents—United States. 2. Political leadership—United
States. I. Title.
JK516.G46 1995
353.03'13—dc20   94-42724
                                                                          CIP

94 95 96 97 9 8 7 6 5 4 3 2 1

To my father

CONTENTS

★★

PREFACE

OFFICEHOLDERS BUT NOT LEADERS

We give the President more work than a man can do, more responsibility than a man should take, more pressure than a man can bear. We abuse him often and rarely praise him. We wear him out, use him up, eat him up. And with all this, Americans have a love for the President that goes beyond loyalty or party nationality; he is ours, and we exercise the right to destroy him.

—John Steinbeck, *America and Americans*

We live in an age of failed leaders. In politics, business, religion, and education, very often those who hold positions of status and power seem to let us down. As our problems grow, our politicians seem to shrink. As circumstances call for leadership, we may instead get pandering and petty rankling. Why? What is wrong?

This book is an effort to understand and explain the failure of the American presidency to meet the needs, expectations, and responsibilities placed upon leaders in the past quarter century. The goal is to evaluate the modern presidents, examine the reasons why their performance has been underwhelming, discuss how presidents might maximize their opportunities for leadership, and ask: can presidents be powerful *and* accountable? The plan of the book follows this format, and it tries to show why our officeholders have not been leaders and how—within the bounds of democratic accountability—presidents can become leaders instead of mere officeholders.

Two decades ago, David Mayhew in *Congress: The Electoral Connection*[1] presented an elegant theory of congressional behavior: Members of Congress seek to maximize their chances for reelection. Since that time Mayhew's "theory" has become all but accepted wisdom in political science. I would like to suggest a "theory" of presidential politics, less elegant but hopefully as persuasive as Mayhew's: *Presidents, facing a system of multiple veto points, seek to maximize power and influence.*[2] Successful presidents use their power and influence to serve the public good. That they usually fail reflects the strength of the president's rivals, the limited resources at his disposal, and the many veto points a president must overcome to gain power. This book is about the roadblocks presidents face, the (limited) avenues of power available to presidents, and how the presidency "fits" into the American political system.

While this theory of presidential behavior focuses on power (the ability to get others to conform to your wishes), in a democratic political system we cannot divorce *power* from *purpose*. The American president is not merely a leader. To be seen as successful, he must be a *democratic leader*. Merely focusing on power might mean that presidents who got their way, for example, Lyndon Johnson and Richard Nixon, were successful presidents. But linking power to purpose in a democratic arena means that success is more than merely accumulating power; it also includes the *ends* to which power is used.

Throughout the book I refer to presidents with the pronoun *he* because all presidents to date have been men. Increasingly women are rising to positions of political power, including chief executives of a number of nations,[3] but thus far, the United States lags behind in affording women equal opportunity to rise to the top position of political leadership.

I am indebted to many people who have been of help in the completion of this work. Typists Margaret Edwards, Bernadette Bernard, and Edna Hastings were extraordinarily cooperative and professional. Research assistants Marija Tenzera, Gabriella Gomez, and Thuy Tran never once complained (to my face, at least) when I sent them back to the library for "more." As always, I owe a debt to friends and colleagues in the Presidency Research Group of the American Political Science Association, who have been welcoming and supportive over the years, especially William Lammers and Thomas Cronin. Seth Thompson, an excellent department chair and good friend, read the entire manuscript and offered sage advice. To all of you, my deepest thanks.

Michael A. Genovese

Chapter 1

★★★

THE DILEMMA OF PRESIDENTIAL LEADERSHIP

Something is very wrong. The presidency, once seen as the great engine of American democracy, now seems to be "the little train that can't!" Where have all the leaders gone?

From the heady days of presidential power in the 1930s, when Franklin D. Roosevelt (FDR) was both powerful and purposeful, we now face a system characterized by gridlock and roadblocks, paralysis and deadlock. When the modern presidency rose out of the ashes of the Great Depression, FDR embodied a president of power, leadership, and ideas. He was a leader who led, not merely an officeholder who presided. But the presidency of the past quarter century has been anything but effective. From Lyndon Johnson to George Bush, the recent presidents have either failed, or performed inadequately. This has created "the crisis of the modern presidency."

The recent presidents have been either strong but pigheadedly wrong (Johnson), strong but corrupt (Nixon and Reagan), weak but honorable (Ford and Carter), or just plain lost in a changing world (Bush). Poor performance characterizes the modern presidents; failure to perform up to expectations is their common bond. For a variety of reasons, the recent presidents have been unable to provide the nation with the leadership necessary to fulfill the Constitution's pledge "to form a more perfect union, establish justice, insure domestic tranquility, provide for the common defense, promote the general welfare, and secure the blessings of liberty to ourselves and our posterity. . . ."

As Phil Williams, an observant British analyst of American politics has noted, "The history of the American presidency since the early 1960s is one of failure, scandal and disaster."[4] Presidency scholar Thomas E. Cronin reminds us that "Presidential frustration is far more the rule than presidential triumph."[5] And political scientists Ted Lowi and Benjamin Ginsberg begin their

1

book *Democrats Return to Power* with this assertion: "Over the past thirty years, the history of the American presidency has been one of disappointment and failure."[6] Presidents of the Republican and Democratic parties, whether from the left or right, have faced a similar fate: the inability to successfully perform the admittedly difficult tasks of the presidency.[7]

The United States has come a long way from its founding, when in one generation, with a population of only 5½ million people, in a tiny emerging nation nestled on the eastern seaboard, this country produced a wealth of great leaders: Washington, Jefferson, Franklin, Hamilton, Madison, Paine, Adams, Henry, Morris, and others. Today, our list of "leaders" includes Lyndon Johnson, Richard Nixon, Gerald Ford, Jimmy Carter, Ronald Reagan, and George Bush; a distinctly undistinguished lot. What has happened? In slightly over 200 years we have gone from the highest mountain of leadership to the deepest valley of despair (with a lot of peaks and valleys in between).

What have our recent presidents wrought? Lyndon Johnson escalated a war in Vietnam, which tore the nation (and the presidency) apart;[8] Richard Nixon, possibly the most corrupt president in the nation's history, gave us the disgrace of Watergate;[9] Gerald Ford was a decent man but politically inept;[10] Jimmy Carter, another decent man, was also politically inept;[11] Ronald Reagan successfully played the role of Wizard of Oz, but when Toto pulled the curtain on his policies, it became clear that he had left the nation in shambles;[12] and George Bush turned out to be a president lost in space, as the dramatic changes of the post–Cold War era left him speechless and idealess.[13]

When three of the past four incumbents lost in their bids for reelection, and six of the past seven presidents left office under circumstances less than desirable, it should be obvious that something is wrong. And yet, when one inquires into the source(s) of these repeated failures, the personalistic explanation is usually offered. While convenient, blaming failure on the individual tells only part of the tale. Other forces of a systemic and institutional sort weigh heavily in our analysis. That the recent presidents have been disappointing seems clear; the multiple reasons for substandard performance may be less evident. Our task is to explore the multiple reasons for presidential inadequacy. Thus, an examination of the ebb and flow of presidential fortunes will give us an insight both into the heady days of presidential greatness and into the decline of presidential performance in the past twenty-five years.

✪ THE DEVOLUTION OF THE PRESIDENCY

Public and scholarly attitudes about the presidency have fluctuated dramatically in the past sixty years. When Franklin D. Roosevelt brought his unique style and political skill to meet the challenge of the Great Depression, then of World War II, the presidency was transformed into a "modern institution," and the White House became the vital center of the American political process. FDR, considered by presidential scholars to be one of the nation's greatest presidents, was a powerful and effective chief executive. Under his leadership the presidency became the prime mover of the American system, and people began to look to the federal government and to the presidency as the nation's problem solver. The federal government had grown, and with it, presidential responsibilities, ending the era in which a president such as Calvin Coolidge could claim that his greatest accomplishment was "minding my own business." Big government led to a big presidency.

Roosevelt was very successful. In fact, he was so successful and so powerful that he transformed the presidency and changed public attitudes about the institution. A "cult of the presidency" began to develop, wherein the office was elevated far beyond the intent of the Framers or the power resources given to the institution. The public began to expect, even demand, that the president *solve* problems. Power became more centralized, expectations focused on the presidency, and the road to power ran directly to the White House.

Roosevelt transformed the presidency. He created expectations of presidential power and leadership that would be imposed on his successors. The "heroic" model of the presidency was established as a result of FDR's leadership, and for the next thirty years, presidential scholars would promote the model as good and necessary. From that point on, all presidents would be in FDR's shadow.[14] As Terry Moe pointed out, after Roosevelt,

> all presidents would be held responsible for addressing every conceivable social problem—however gargantuan . . . intractable . . . far removed from the president's actual sphere of power—and they would be expected, through legislative leadership and executive control of the administrative apparatus of the government, to take action.[15]

And Roosevelt did not disappoint. Elected president four times, FDR was powerful, popular, and charismatic. He got the system moving. Increasingly, the presidency became more powerful, more personalized, and the United States was transformed into a presidency-centered system. It was in this era that what political scientist Thomas E. Cronin called the "Superman" or textbook image of the presidency took root.[16] Roosevelt planted the seeds that would grow into a view of the institution of the presidency as the seat of power, benevolence, and wisdom. As Robert Spitzer notes, "Roosevelt would become the yardstick by which every future president would be measured."[17] High standards indeed. Roosevelt guided the nation through the depression, led the nation to the eve of victory in World War II, and utterly transformed the presidency. Roosevelt was a great president, but the myth of FDR took on even greater stature. An inflated view of Roosevelt passed for fact in popular and scholarly conceptions of the presidency. He was never really as powerful as he is remembered. But if this FDR is the yardstick of measurement for presidential success, could any mere mortal be expected to live up to such Herculean standards?

Could this wisdom, virtue, and power extend beyond one man and be embodied in an institution? When FDR died in office toward the end of World War II, his vice president, the diminutive Harry S Truman, became president. How could Truman fill the shoes of FDR? How could this interloper presume to grasp and use the power of this grand institution?

Truman assumed the presidency in the final days of World War II. In an effort to hasten an end to the war, he ordered the atomic bomb(s) to be dropped in Japan. After the war, it was Truman who devised the "containment" policy toward the Soviet Union—a policy which each succeeding president would follow, more or less, until 1989 and the end of the Cold War. It was Truman who established the Marshall Plan, or European Recovery Program, helped establish the North Atlantic Treaty Organization (NATO), and led the United States back to a postwar domestic economic revival. It was also under Truman that the Korean War began.

To the surprise of most of his contemporaries, Truman became a very effective president (though his popularity could never match that of FDR, and it would be only after he left office that his contribution was fully appreciated). Truman created a sense often expressed in this way: "Surely if *he* can do the job, there must be something inherent in the office that brings out greatness in even the most common of men." Thus was born the "FDR halo," which could be passed down from president to president, a kind of magic that seemed to confer special powers on the occupant of the White House.

When Dwight D. Eisenhower (Ike), a Republican, became president in 1953, he lent a bipartisan air to the majesty of the office. While not an activist president, Ike did manage to exert a hidden-hand type of leadership[18] in an era when the public seemed anxious to take a break from the hurly-burly world of politics. After all, the United States had been through a depression in the 1930s, a world war in the 1940s, a nascent cold war in the late forties and early fifties, and by the Eisenhower era, the American people wanted a rest. Ike, with a low-key, almost apolitical style, gave them what they wanted. Ike was amazingly popular, especially for a president who seemed to do so little, and his popularity extended across the entire eight years of his tenure.

Eisenhower, the great military hero who had served as commander of U.S. forces in Europe, had a rather limited agenda as president. In general terms he sought peace abroad and prosperity at home. During his presidency, the Korean War ended and a massive interstate highway-building program began. While his substantive accomplishments may have been a bit thin, Eisenhower inspired trust and confidence and helped bring about stability and calm in the nation.

If the FDR halo seemed to be in limbo during the Eisenhower years, Ike's successor was determined to pull it out of mothballs. John F. Kennedy, the Camelot president, wanted an activist administration, and after eight years of Eisenhower, the public seemed ready for action. But try as he might, President Kennedy's legislative proposals often fell prey to unresponsive leaders in Congress. Stymied by an intransigent Congress, which took the system of checks and balances quite seriously, the Kennedy legislative record was at best mixed. The first Roman Catholic ever to be elected president, Kennedy won the presidency by a razor-thin margin in 1960. Kennedy presided over the Bay of Pigs fiasco in Cuba, placed military advisors in Vietnam, and successfully led the nation through the Cuban Missile Crisis. But his ambitious and progressive domestic initiatives often were blocked by a Congress controlled by conservatives in his own party. Kennedy did achieve tax cuts, which stimulated economic growth, and he started the Peace Corps and placed civil rights reform on the presidential agenda, but overall he was stymied by a reluctant Congress.

This led to grumblings among the public and scholars: "How can the Congress stand in the way of progress? . . . There are too many checks on the presidency. . . . We need *more* power for the president" went the chants. If the presidency was good and just, it also deserved to be strong, and it was the Congress that stood in the way.

The untimely death of John Kennedy in 1963 left unattained the legislative agenda of the slain president. But his successor, Lyndon Johnson, was a legislative genius who, exploiting the opportunity, managed not only to pass most of the Kennedy proposals that lay dormant but even to expand Kennedy's activist program and promote a more ambitious social agenda, which he called the "Great Society." In 1964 and 1965, Johnson passed bill after bill, far surpassing anything his critics thought possible. It seemed the FDR halo and Camelot had merged to produce a protean presidency of power and purpose. We were a nation intoxicated by presidential power.

The FDR halo was truly revived. Lyndon Johnson brought the strong-presidency model back to life. The public could breathe easier knowing that a strong president—a superman—was once again at the helm. Johnson's success confirmed the heroic-presidency model. It was proof positive that the strong presidency was a good presidency, that more presidential power meant greater public good. The public injected another dose of the drug of strong leadership, and it felt good. The public once again became sedated by the strong-presidency model. They placed their trust in the president, invested their hopes in the office, saw the president as powerful, good, and trustworthy. What political scientists have called a "Hallowed Be the President" (1932–1966) attitude consumed the public (see Table 1.1).[19]

But it would soon prove to be misplaced trust, because the seeds of the "Imperial Presidency" were planted in this period, and it would not be long before public trust turned to disdain. If the era of the cult of the presidency led to the public's and academics' (who probably should have known better) demanding more (unchecked) power for presidents and placing too much trust in the institution, the harsh lessons of political reality would soon haunt the all-too-trusting and unwary people in both camps.

If the public suspended its disbelief and almost blindly placed its faith in the strong-presidency model, why did academics so easily go along? Of course, there were voices in the wilderness, warning of the dangers of unchecked presidential power,[20] but in general, scholars and the public were equally intoxicated by the strong presidency. Richard Neustadt's seminal work, *Presidential Power*,[21] first published in 1960, is just one of many examples of a noted scholar encouraging presidents to maximize power and pursue the goal of presidency-centered politics.

Scholars were as captivated as anyone at the prospect of a strong president leading the fragmented system to new heights, overcoming the chains of the checks and balances, and achieving mighty and good ends. A sampling of

Table 1.1 MODERN VIEWS OF THE PRESIDENCY

1932–1966: "Hallowed Be the President"

- FDR halo
- New Deal to JFK's Camelot, to LBJ's Great Society
- Cult of the presidency
- "Superman" image
- Seeds of Imperial Presidency

1967–1974: "Deliver Us from Presidents"

- Presidents above the Law/President as King
- LBJ and Vietnam
- RMN and Watergate
- Imperial Presidency
- Era of cynicism spawned

1975–1980: "Blessed Are the Meek"

- Presidency-curbing period
- Ford and Carter, weak leaders
- Imperiled Presidency
- Hangover from cult of the presidency

1981–1986: "Search for a Savior"

- Wizard of Oz in the White House
- Return of Imperial Presidency
- Reagan's Iran-Contra scandal
- U.S. as world's largest debtor nation
- Revenge of the strong-presidency model

1986–?: "Where there is no vision, the people perish"

- Bush's visionless leadership
- "Wimpyman" image
- U.S. as a declining world power
- President as passive observer
- Clinton's "I feel your pain" leadership

quotes from the classic *The American Presidency* by Clinton Rossiter, first published in 1956, gives an indication of the status and esteem in which even the conservative Rossiter held the presidency.

> Few nations have solved so simply and yet grandly the problem of finding and maintaining an office or state that embodies their majesty and reflects their character. . . .
> There is virtually no limit to what the President can do if he does it for democratic ends and by democratic means. . . .
> He reigns, but he also rules; he symbolizes the people, but he also runs their government. . . .

Gulliver goes to Washington

BOBDOLENAGIANS, I PRESUME?

The President is not a Gulliver immobilized by ten thousand tiny cords, nor even a Prometheus chained to a rock of frustration. He is, rather, a kind of magnificent lion who can roam widely and do great deeds so long as he does not try to break loose from his broad reservation.[22]

And Rossiter writes that the American presidency is "one of the few truly successful institutions created by men in their endless quest for the blessings of free government." He concludes by writing:

It is, finally, an office of freedom. The Presidency is a standing reproach to those petty doctrinaires who insist that executive power is inherently undemocratic; for, to the exact contrary, it has been more responsive to the needs and dreams of giant democracy than any other office or institution in the whole mosaic of American life. It is no less a reproach to those easy generalizers who think that Lord Acton had the very last word on the corrupting effects of power, for, again, to the contrary, his doctrine finds small confirmation in the history of the Presidency. The vast power of this office has not been "poison," as Henry Adams wrote in scorn; rather, it has elevated often and corrupted never, chiefly because those who held it recognized the true source of the power and were ennobled by the knowledge.[23]

Rossiter is not alone in his celebration of the presidency and presidential power. In 1960, Richard Neustadt publishes the influential *Presidential Power: The*

Politics of Leadership. For Neustadt, a strong president was essential in order to overcome the natural lethargy of a system of "separated institutions sharing power." Neustadt writes:

> The contributions that a President can make to government are indispensable. Assuming that he knows what power is and wants it, those contributions cannot help but be forthcoming in some measure as by-products of his search for personal influence. In a relative but real sense one can say of a President what Eisenhower's first Secretary of Defense once said of General Motors: what is good for the country is good for the President and vice versa.[24]

We can thus see the intellectual origins of what Thomas E. Cronin would call the "textbook presidency," a Superman who was good, powerful, and essential. After examining standard civics textbooks of the 1960s, Cronin discovered an idealized view of the presidency.[25] This textbook version of the presidency romanticized the office and heaped honor upon the president. The president was presented as Superman, able to leap tall separations of power in a single bound.

In 1960, Herman Finer presents this view in a combined religious and heroic vision of the presidency, not only as "the incarnation of the American people in a sacrament resembling that in which the wafer and the wine are seen to be the body and blood of Christ" but also as belonging "rightfully to the offspring of a titan and Minerva husbanded by Mars."[26] In 1965, James MacGregor Burns echoes this view in secular terms when he writes in *Presidential Government* that "the stronger we make the Presidency, the more we strengthen democratic procedures."[27] And in 1967, Grant McConnell writes that "to ask what is to become of the presidency is to ask what is to become of the entire American political order."[28]

This presidency-centered model, which came to dominate thinking, was more than an operating style of government; it was also a *philosophy* of governing. It was an operating style in that it promoted a system of government in which the president was to direct or lead the people and the other branches of government from a perch of great power. It was a philosophy of government in that it legitimized a stronger central government that took power away from the other branches, and perhaps even more important, it took power from the people and vested responsibility in the hands of government (the president) to solve problems. Thus it diminished the democratic responsibility placed in the people (a Jeffersonian goal) and promoted responsibility and power in the leadership class (a Hamiltonian goal). It also failed to recognize the potential danger of the heroic-leadership model.

Lyndon Johnson's remarkable legislative achievements in the wake of John Kennedy's tragic assassination confirmed for many the wisdom of the strong-presidency model: the presidency was seen as the seat of wisdom, virtue, and effectiveness, and Lyndon Johnson looked like a Mount Rushmore type of leader. After all, was it not presidential leadership that brought about economic strength, international clout, expanding social services? More power to the presidency, it was argued, to do more good things.

Lyndon Johnson was a legislative genius. In 1965 and 1966, he and the 89th Congress passed an astounding array of bills: Medicare, Medicaid, the Civil Rights Act, the War on Poverty, the Air Pollution Control Act, the Elementary and Secondary Education Act; and they created the Departments of Transportation and of Housing and Urban Development.

But just when the public was lulled into a false sense of complacency and security concerning the benevolence of presidential power, things began to change. And they changed quickly and dramatically. It started with Vietnam.

U.S. involvement in Vietnam began quietly, escalated slowly, and eventually led to tragedy.[29] By 1966, the United States was engaged in a war that it could not win and from which it could not (honorably) withdraw. It was a "presidential war," and it brought the Johnson administration to its knees.[30]

As U.S. involvement escalated, and as victory seemed further and further away, blame was placed squarely on the shoulders of President Johnson. Although the Constitution gives the power to declare war to the Congress, in practice since the Truman administration and the "Korean Conflict," presidents have often acted unilaterally in this regard. By the time Johnson came to office, presidents had been setting policy in Vietnam for twenty years, unencumbered by the Congress. As U.S. involvement escalated, it was the president who was calling the shots. The tragedy of Lyndon Johnson is that after such a sterling start, after such great success, the blunder of Vietnam would overwhelm him and the nation. From such great heights the president fell to such tragic depths. The nation was torn apart. The glue that bound Americans together had lost its adhesiveness, and in its place, divisiveness and conflict overtook the nation. The strong presidency, so long seen as the savior of the American system, now seemed too powerful, too dangerous, too unchecked—in short, a threat. After years of hearing calls for "more power to the president," by the late 1960s the plea was to rein in the overly powerful "monster" in the White House.

It was a rude awakening. All the hopes, all the trust, all the expectations that had been entrusted to the presidency were being shattered. Johnson was compelled not to seek reelection in 1968 when faced with the near certainty of electoral defeat. But that was not the end of it. His successor was to degrade the nation's image of the presidency even further.

If the Vietnam War was tearing our nation apart, Johnson's successor, Richard M. Nixon, would continue to plunge the presidency and the nation toward the depths of division and degradation. Promising in the 1968 campaign to "bring us together," Nixon only brought the nation together in the collective shame of massive corruption and pettiness, when the president of the United States was named an "unindicted co-conspirator" by the federal grand jury during the crisis of Watergate.[31]

From the start of his administration, Richard Nixon faced "divided government"; that is, the White House was controlled by one party, the Republicans, but the Congress was controlled by the Democrats. This made the already difficult task of governing even more problematic, and the divided government degenerated progressively into divisive government. Seeing little hope for working with a Congress controlled by his "enemies," Nixon attempted to govern by executive fiat and administrative discretion. It was a strategy doomed from the start.

Nixon extended, then ended the war in Vietnam. This led to a stunning reelection landslide victory in 1972. From then on it was downhill. Nixon's was the most corrupt administration in U.S. history, and the president himself was deeply involved in the crimes of Watergate.[32] With the institution of the presidency already weakened by the tragedy of the Vietnam War, the revelations of corruption, referred to under the umbrella term "Watergate," led to a further diminution of presidential prestige.

In July 1972, during Nixon's campaign for a second term, agents for his reelection committee had been arrested for burglary at the Democratic party headquarters in the Washington, D.C., Watergate apartment building, after an attempt to wiretap telephones there. This precipitating event—which led almost a year later to the special Senate hearings called to investigate Watergate—proved to be only a minor part of the widespread corruption within the Nixon administration.

The revelations of Watergate stunned the nation. The president and a number of his top aides had been involved in a variety of crimes and dirty tricks (e.g., obstruction of justice, extortion, burglary, cover-ups, paying of hush money, etc.). What shocked the nation was the level of direct presidential involvement in many of these crimes.

Nixon, the only U.S. president forced to resign his office, did have several significant foreign policy achievements—the opening of relations with China, détente with the Soviet Union, drawing the war in Vietnam to a conclusion—and he was somewhat progressive in domestic affairs. But all of this is overshadowed by the crimes and corruption of Watergate. Nixon was forced to relinquish his office when faced with the certainty of impeachment by the House and conviction by the Senate.

A major transformation began to take place. As a result first of Vietnam, then of Watergate, our Superman became an Imperial President. Historian Arthur M. Schlesinger, Jr., in his influential book *The Imperial Presidency*,[33] argues that the abuse of power by presidents threatened the constitutional integrity of the U.S. system of government. With the rise of the president's war powers and the increased secrecy surrounding presidential initiatives, the president was usurping and abusing power and acting above the law. Cronin's Superman—savior of the people—became Schlesinger's enemy of the people. The presidency had become a danger to the republic, using its powers not for the public good but for self-aggrandizement. A new image of the presidency developed. Superman was no longer on the side of the people; the power of the institution, which we thought would be used for good, also granted the bearer of this power a capacity to do wrong. Historian Marcus Cunliffe was compelled to call the presidency a "Frankenstein monster."[34]

Watergate turned out to be the final nail in the coffin of the unambiguous acceptance of the strong-presidency model. The twin effects of Vietnam and Watergate led to an era of deep cynicism regarding politics and the presidency. Scholars and the public began to condemn the "excesses" of presidential power characterized as the Imperial Presidency,[35] and to call for a corralling of a presidency perceived as acting above the law. It was a presidency-curbing, if not presidency-bashing, period, an era of "Deliver Us from Presidents" (1967–1974).

As a reaction against the excesses of power (or should we say "the mistakes"?) in the Johnson and Nixon presidencies, the Congress attempted to reassert its power by taking a series of presidency-curbing steps, the most notable being the passage of the War Powers Act, which attempted (with little subsequent success) to curb the president's war powers. The presidency-curbing era also ushered in a period in which the public did an about-face regarding their trust in and support of presidents and the presidency. If blind faith had characterized the Hallowed Be the President era (1932–1966), blind *distrust* characterized the Deliver Us from Presidents period. Any and all presidential acts were suspect; virtually no support was given for presidential initiatives; and a weak-presidency model (though not a strong-Congress model) prevailed. In the midterm election of 1974, a new breed of activist Democrats was elected to the Congress. Weaned not on FDR's greatness but on Johnson's and Nixon's excesses, this new generation of legislators was less deferential to presidents, less willing to bow to claims of presidential prerogative, and more willing to directly challenge presidents. As a result, the legislative initiatives of Presidents Ford and Carter would fall victim to the Congress's revised, more suspicious attitude toward presidential power.

If the Johnson and Nixon years revealed an Imperial Presidency, the Ford and Carter years revealed an Imperiled Presidency. The cult of the presidency gave way to revulsion and distrust. It was a period characterized as "Blessed Are the Meek" (1975–1980). In 1980, Vice President Walter Mondale referred to the presidency as "the fire hydrant of the nation."[36]

After Vice President Spiro Agnew resigned the office in 1973 and pleaded nolo contendere to charges of tax evasion, Richard Nixon appointed Gerald Ford vice president. Following Nixon's resignation in August of 1974, Ford became America's first "unelected" president. Shortly after taking office, Ford granted his predecessor a "full free and absolute pardon" for any crimes he may have committed as president. In Congress and among the public, suspicions persisted that Ford had pardoned Nixon for political or personal expediency. In this cynical atmosphere, President Ford's ability to govern foundered and he quickly became a caretaker president.

In his brief time as president, Gerald Ford did help restore the nation to a period of relative calm, and he helped slowly to restore the integrity of the presidency in a post-Watergate era. But the cynicism born of Vietnam and Watergate persisted, and Ford fell as one of its many victims.

In the aftermath of Watergate and the Nixon pardon, the public elected a relative unknown to the White House, Jimmy Carter. As president, Carter attempted to demythologize the presidency. He recognized that dramatic changes were taking place in the world and that America's power was declining relative to the robust hegemony the United States had enjoyed in the immediate aftermath of World War II. Carter tried to get the nation to adjust to these changing power circumstances, but he was unable to persuade a public hooked on consumerism that they had to settle for less.[37] When American hostages were taken in Iran, Carter seemed weak and paralyzed. The nation cried out for strong leadership, and Carter could not answer this call.

Like Gerald Ford, Jimmy Carter was a man of great decency but (again like Ford) limited political acumen. He faced a presidency-bashing age with great dignity but insufficient skill. He could not get the Congress controlled by his own party to pass his legislative agenda, and when events around the world came crashing down upon him, Carter seemed helpless and ineffective.[38]

President Carter's major success was the Camp David peace accords between Egypt and Israel. He also focused world attention on human rights and achieved civil service reform. But when double-digit inflation and soaring interest rates combined with Carter's seeming helplessness in the face of Iranian student radicals' taking hostage fifty-two Americans, Carter's presidency seemed doomed.

After a period of leaderless drift, the nation began to forget about the problems of presidential power, and a hunger for leadership reemerged. Problems accumulated, and the nation's "leaders" seemed powerless in the face of these hardships. The urge for the strong-presidency model reclaimed center stage, and a new era, the "Search for a Savior" (1980–1986), appeared.

The people wanted a strong leader, one who could solve problems, one who would flex America's muscles. Enter Ronald Reagan, a presidential knight in shining armor. Reagan seemed to be everything Ford and Carter weren't: strong, self-assured, a leader. He made grand promises, spoke in grand terms, built expectations high. He attempted to return to an era of American grandeur.

Reagan took Washington by storm. Claiming a bold mandate and focusing on several key economic items, Reagan managed to get most of his top agenda items enacted into law. But after an impressive start, Reagan faltered. Initial success in dealing with Congress gave way to frustration and defeat. The president could not overcome the systems roadblocks, and unwilling to accept the limits placed upon the office, he and members of his administration went beyond the law and abused power.[39]

Reagan was not what he seemed. He appeared strong but was weak; looked like he was in control but was often manipulated by handlers or his wife; promised greatness but left the American economy and infrastructure in a shambles. For Reagan, appearance did not match reality. He was a Wizard of Oz president. He gave the appearance of strength and power, but when the curtain was pulled away, a weak, rather pathetic figure was revealed. He ruled by illusion and by manipulation of the blind faith placed in him by the public.[40] To compound matters, Reagan, like Nixon, displayed a distinct lack of respect for the law and attempted to impose a new Imperial Presidency,[41] and in the end his presidency was nearly destroyed by the Iran-Contra scandal.

Reagan's engaging personality and ready wit helped make him popular, and while his borrow-borrow, spend-spend approach to policy may have added to America's military might, it also left the nation on the brink of economic insolvency. The United States went from being the world's largest creditor/lender nation in 1980 to becoming the world's largest debtor/borrower nation in 1988. Thus, when opportunity presented itself, Reagan was unable to convert the collapse of Soviet Communism to American advantage. The United States declined while Europe and Japan grew.[42] Reagan was successful at achieving early legislative victories, attaining the largest tax cuts in U.S. history, and he helped reduce the inflation rate. In foreign affairs his major accomplishment was signing the Intermediate range Nuclear Forces (INF) treaty with the Soviet Union. But his administration was marred by record budget deficits, scandal, and the Iran-Contra affair.

After Reagan, scholars and the public seemed once again thoroughly confused as to what limits to place on the presidency. The roller-coaster ride that alternated between strong and weak models of presidential power left the people feeling somewhat schizophrenic about it. (Anyone who wasn't schizophrenic just wasn't thinking clearly.) These dramatic shifts in attitudes about the presidency have led presidential scholar Michael Nelson to note that "the sheer velocity of the turnover in these models since the 1960s would seem to indicate that the best single-word description of how scholars evaluate the presidency is 'confusion.'"[43] This confusion has led to the current era, a "Where there is no vision, the people perish" period (1986–?).

The presidency under George Bush was in a state of suspended animation. Bush, a man of uncompromising grayness, was a manager at a time when the nation needed a leader. The end of the Cold War opened a window of opportunity to exert creative leadership. But Bush was shackled by a vastly depleted resource base (the legacy of Reagan's economic mismanagement) and an intellectual cupboard that was bare (no vision for a post–Cold War future). Bush often seemed a passive observer in a dramatically changing world. If the presidency of the Hallowed Be the President era could be classified as "Superman,"[44] the presidency in this era looked more like "Wimpyman."[45]

Bush was at his best when he had a clear goal to achieve (e.g., the Gulf War), a goal imposed upon him by events. But when it came time for him to choose, to set priorities, to decide upon a direction, he floundered. As conservative columnist George Will commented, "When the weight of the [presidency] is put upon a figure as flimsy as George Bush, the presidency buckles. . . ."[46]

George Bush had the greatest résumé in Washington, having served two terms in the House of Representatives, as ambassador to the United Nations, chairman of the Republican National Committee, chief of the U.S. Liaison Office in China, director of the CIA, and as vice president, but he served as a managerial president, not a leader. In a time that cried out for vision, Bush seemed paralyzed. He seemed to want to be president so as to add another impressive notch on his résumé. There was no clear aspiration to accomplish any grand goals. Bush's successes include the Persian Gulf War and a winding down of the Cold War, but his failures—inability to build on the concept of a New World Order or to counter rising deficits, no domestic agenda to speak of, and a stand-pat attitude as the economy tumbled—opened the door to Bush's opponents in the 1992 election. When it came time for the public to render judgment on President Bush, it chose another relative unknown over George Bush.

In January 1993, Bill Clinton—who had been a successful governor of Arkansas but was an outsider to Washington politics and little known before the presidential campaign—began his administration with an ambitious set of campaign pledges and an economy creeping toward recovery. According to Lowi and Ginsberg, President Clinton is "haunted by two ghosts—the legacies of Ronald Reagan and James Madison."[47] The ghost of Reagan can be seen in the enormous debt Reagan left to his successors; that of Madison can be seen in the system of checks and balances, of limited and shared powers—of a separation rather than a fusion of governmental power.

Clinton has had other problems as well. In addition to his lack of Washington experience, he won only 43 percent of the popular vote for president in a three-way race, running behind virtually every member of Congress in their districts. He was not granted the typical "honeymoon" period. And yet, Clinton's youth and energy, his native intelligence and ability to connect with people, and having his party control Congress may in the long run work in his favor. At the end of his first year in office, the record was at best mixed. He was given low marks for his timing and method of pursuing the goal to allow gays to serve in the military; the "character" issue continued to plague him; he failed to get Congress to pass his economic stimulus package; and revelations of the Whitewater scandal have continued to hound both President and Mrs. Clinton. On the plus side, Clinton succeeded in passing the North American Free Trade Agreement (NAFTA), a budget resolution, and the Brady Act to help control guns. Overall, his record in getting Congress to pass his legislation is the highest—at 86.4 percent—since LBJ's 88 percent in 1964. Of course, several key questions remain unanswered, including the fate of health care legislation, his anticrime proposals, welfare reform, and a host of foreign policy issues such as Bosnia, Haiti, the Middle East, Russia, and other trouble spots.

Would he, could he, perform better than his immediate predecessors? If past is prelude, President Clinton will have an enormously difficult time living up to the very high expectations invested in the presidency. We ask, even demand, much of our presidents, but rarely do we give them the tools to succeed. Our presidents usually fail because they are set up to fail. Larger systemic forces usually guarantee that presidents will not be able to perform up to our high expectations.

The 1970s brought about the "dwarfing of the presidency," the early 1980s brought on a "they might be giants but turned out to be pygmies" period, and the Bush years seemed to constitute a period of "stealth leadership" or presidential sclerosis. Following the public's repeated disappointments—with presidents who didn't or weren't able to keep their campaign promises and who time after time turned in substandard performances—its lowered perceptions of the presidency were combined with an equally reduced view of government's overall capacity to function. In effect, the people felt like Charlie Brown in the Peanuts cartoon that appears every fall. In it, Charlie Brown and Lucy are in a field, and Lucy, holding a football in place on the ground, insists that Charlie run up and kick it. Charlie, who has gone through this every year, demurs, knowing that if past is prelude, Lucy will pull the ball away at the last minute and Charlie will fall flat on his rear. But Lucy insists, promising Charlie that she will not pull the ball away, and finally Charlie gives in. He runs up, goes to kick the ball, and—of course—at the last second Lucy pulls the ball away and Charlie falls flat on his butt. Every election, candidates promise salvation; every election, the public hesitates but eventually places its hopes and trust in one man; and every year, the football ends up getting pulled away and the public ends up flat on its collective butt. The end result is failed policies, voter cynicism, and a backlog of unsolved problems. Presidents just aren't up to the task of governing.

Presidential hopefuls will, during campaigns, promise much. Do they deliver? In a study of presidential promises kept and unkept, political scientist Jeff Fishel found that none of the modern presidents was able to fully keep half of his promises. The president who fully kept the highest percentage of his campaign promises was Jimmy Carter at 47 percent, followed by Lyndon Johnson at 45 percent. If one includes promises fully and partially kept, the presidents rank as follows:

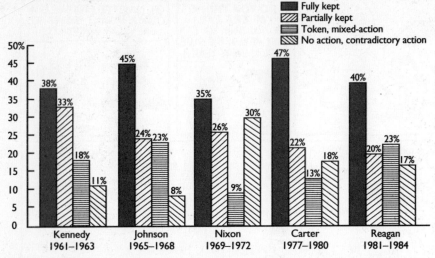

Source: Adopted from Jeff Fishel, *Presidents & Promises* (Washington, D.C.: CQ Press, 1985).

Figure 1.1   Percentage of Presidential Campaign Promises Kept, Kennedy to Reagan.

1.	Kennedy	71%
2.	Carter	69%
3.	Johnson	69%
4.	Nixon	61%
5.	Reagan	60%

The president who acted least on promises or engaged most in contradictory action was Richard Nixon at 30 percent (see Figure 1.1 for full details).

✪ FAILING THE LEADERSHIP TEST

What does this all add up to? The history of the modern presidency (the presidents who have served for the past twenty-five years) could, I argue, be seen as a period of failure or disappointment. The United States alternated between weak leaders (Ford and Carter), corrupt or abusive leaders (Johnson, Nixon, and Reagan), or lost and directionless leaders (Bush). There is not one great leader, not one good leader, and barely an above average leader in the lot.

But is it fair to characterize the presidents of the past twenty-five years as "failed" or substandard leaders? Is that not a bit harsh? Couldn't we say "mediocre" instead? While in some respects it might be better to say that the modern presidents, taken as a group, have been mediocre, an unvarnished examination of their performance leads us to admit that they have been disappointing—that they have failed to live up to their own inflated promises, to our high expectations, or even to more modest standards of acceptability.

Not one of the presidents under examination left office under terms he would have preferred. Each of them departed under a cloud of shame or of bitter disappointment. These discredited presidents: Lyndon Johnson, who was compelled not to even seek reelection because of the problem of Vietnam; Richard Nixon, who resigned in disgrace because of the crimes of Watergate; Ford and Carter, who seemed totally overwhelmed by the job and were defeated at the polls; Ronald Reagan (popular but inept), who left office with the Iran-Contra scandal damaging his image; and George Bush, yet another one-term disappointment—all of them left office under unfavorable conditions, and not one had been a truly successful president.

In examining the administrations of the modern presidents (see Table 1.2), several patterns stand out. First, we note the absence of strongly ideological presidents. Of the eleven presidents listed in the table, only two have had strongly held ideological convictions (FDR and Reagan). Most of these presidents have been centrist in their political orientations. Second, in recent years we have seen the Republicanization of the White House—between 1969 and 1993, the Republicans have controlled the White House twenty of the twenty-four years—and the Democratization of the Congress. This institutionalizes divided government. Third, Democrats have tended to be more activist in domestic and economic policy, and Republicans more restrained (Reagan being the exception). Fourth, in foreign policy, all except Clinton have adopted, more or less, a Cold War approach to dealing with the world. Finally, as noted, recent presidents are not a highly regarded group of leaders. Of the last four presidents (Nixon through Reagan) who are ranked in the Murray-Blessing poll of U.S. historians, the combined average ranking of 28 (out of 37) would place them at the bottom of the Below Average category among the presidents included in the poll. By contrast, the first four listed in the table (FDR thru Kennedy) received a combined average ranking of 8.5, the Near Great category

One could conclude, then, that "the system" isn't working: The combined effects of gridlock, stalemate, voter desertion, excessive expectations, demand overload, widespread public cynicism, and ineffectual leadership have produced a clearly negative trend in the public's image of the presidency. Presidents now seem unable to navigate the choppy waters of America's brand of representative democracy. From both the political left and right, there is a general perception that something is wrong with the institution of the presidency. There is widespread agreement that the presidency—once seen as the instrument of political change in America—has not been able to accomplish the task of leadership. It was a short trip from Superman to Wimpyman.

Now, instead of being viewed as a powerful institution, the presidency is being portrayed as limited or weak. Instead of asking "Toward what ends should a president lead?" we begin to ask "Can a president lead?" From our view of Superman to that of the Imperial or Imperiled or Wimpyman presidency, we have made a complete turnabout. From the cult of the presidency we have shifted to the shackled presidency, from Superman to Nowhere Man.

.2 THE MODERN PRESIDENCY

President	Ideology	Background: Congress (C) Executive (E)	Party	Congressional Majority	Electoral Majority
F. Roosevelt	Liberal	E Gov.	D	D	'32: 57.4–39.6 '36: 60.8–36.5 '40: 54.7–44.8 '44: 53.4–45.9
H. Truman	Pragmatic Liberal	C E/VP	D	R/D	'48: 49.5–45.1
D. Eisenhower	Pragmatic Conservative	NA	R	R/D	'52: 55.5–44.4 '56: 57.4–42.0
J. Kennedy	Pragmatic Liberal	C	D	D	'60: 49.7–49.5
L. Johnson	Pragmatic Liberal	C E/VP	D	D	'64: 61.1–38.5
R. Nixon	Pragmatic Conservative	C E/VP	R	D	'68: 43.4–42.7 '72: 60.7–37.5
G. Ford	Pragmatic Conservative	C E/VP	R	D	NA
J. Carter	Pragmatic Liberal	E Gov.	D	D	'76: 50.1–48.0
R. Reagan	Conservative	E Gov.	R	R/D	'80: 50.7–41.0 '84: 58.8–40.6
G. Bush	Pragmatic Conservative	C E/VP	R	D	'88: 53.4–45.6
W. Clinton (1st year)	Pragmatic Liberal	E Gov.	D	D	'92: 43–38–19

Popular Support	Domestic Policy	Economic Policy	Foreign Policy	Management Style	Major Accomplishments	Rating
Steady/High	Activist/ New Deal	Activist/ New Deal	WWII	High Involvement; Competitive Approach	New Deal Legislation; WWII Victory	#2; Great
Moderate to Low	Activist/ Fair Deal	Activist/ Fair Deal	WWII; Cold War Containment	Mixed/Mixed	Cold War Containment; Return to Postwar Economics; NATO	#8; Near Great
Steady/High	Restraint	Restraint	Cold War	Mixed/ Hierarchical	Ended Korean War; Return to Normality	#11; Above Average
Steady/High	Activist/ New Frontier	Activist/ Growth Policy	Cold War	High/Spokes-in-Wheel	Cuban Missile Crisis; Nuclear Test Ban Treaty; Peace Corps	#13; Above Average
High to Low	Activist/ Great Society	Activist/ Growth Policy	Cold War; Vietnam	High/Spokes-in-Wheel	Great Society; Civil Rights	#10; Above Average
Moderate to Low	Restraint	Restraint/ Wage & Price Controls	Cold War; Détente	High/ Hierarchical	Open Relations w/China; Détente w/Soviet Union; SALT I Treaty	#35; Failure
Moderate to Low	Restraint	Restraint/ Veto	Cold War	Mixed/ Spokes-in-Wheel	Return to Calm in Post-Watergate Age	#24; Low Average
Moderate to Low	Mixed	Mixed	Cold War; Human Rights	High/Spokes-in-Wheel	Egypt-Israeli Treaty; Human Rights	#25; Low Average
High to Moderate	Mixed/ Christian Crusade	Activist/ Supply Side	Cold War; Détente	Aloof/ Multiple	End of Cold War; INF Treaty	#28; Below Average
High to Moderate	Restraint	Restraint	Manage Decline New World Order?	Mixed/ Spokes-in-Wheel	Gulf War; New World Order	?
Year One: Moderate to Low	Activist	Activist	Lack of Direction	High Involvement	NAFTA; Brady Act; Crime Bill; Haiti	?

A decade ago, presidency scholar Harold M. Barger noted a trend that, if anything, is even more pronounced today:

> We live in a time of disposable presidents. Some might insist that this is not so unusual because our society is a disposable society. But presidents were not always so dispensable, and the reasons why the White House, which once symbolized stability and continuity, has lately become a revolving door for incumbents is only partly answered by our nation's tendency to consume and then discard. Americans dispose of one president after another because no recent incumbent has been able to measure up to the office. No incumbent measures up because an immense gulf has opened between what people have come to expect and what presidents can realistically deliver.[48]

Barger calls the presidency "impossible," arguing that, both at home and abroad, presidents are unable to deliver on promises or meet public expectations.

> The impossible presidency is the imperial presidency turned upside down. The imperial presidency was feared for what seemed to be unbridled powers over American military and foreign policy, as well as for a frequently callous disregard for the will of Congress. The impossible presidency is a matter of concern because of its seeming inability to exert American power convincingly anywhere in the world, as well as for its incapacity to provide leadership in domestic policymaking.[49]

In less than twenty years, Superman—upon whom few checks seemed to exist—was replaced by presidents upon whom the system of checks and balances was resumed with a vengeance. Images of failure, limitation, and weakness dominate the new presidential literature. We can choose between Harold Barger's description of "the impossible presidency" and Theodore Sorensen's of "political gridlock" or "all checks and no balances." James L. Sundquist writes of "failed presidents," James M. Burns of "deadlock," and Peter Smithers of "presidential paralysis." Hugh Heclo discusses the "illusion of presidential government," Thomas M. Franck the "tethered presidency," Paul Light the "no win" presidency, and Aaron Wildavsky "the beleagured presidency." Thomas E. Cronin sees an "imperiled" presidency, and Godfrey Hodgson calls the modern presidency "impotent." As Hodgson states, "Never has so powerful a leader been so impotent to do what he wants to do, what he is pledged to do, what he is expected to do, and what he knows he must do."[50]

After "presidential" wars and scandals, after the resurgent Congress, after the public's withdrawal of support, presidential scholars became more sensitive to the weakness of presidential power and to the limitations, checks, and constraints placed on it: so many checks, so few balances; so many roadblocks, so few resources; so much separation, so little power. Institutional impotence, not power, has become part of the new textbook presidency.

We tend to judge presidents on the basis of four factors: (1) the scope of the *problems* they faced; (2) their *efforts* (actions) and *intentions* (vision) in dealing with these problems; (3) what they were able to *accomplish*; and (4) the long-term *results* of their actions. By these measures, the recent presidents have disappointed us.

If we compare our sample of presidents with the roster of earlier presidents, we find, according to professional judgments, that none of the modern presidents after LBJ is highly regarded. In the Murray and Blessing survey[51] asking historians to rank the presidents, no modern president stands in the Great category (which includes Lincoln, F. D. Roosevelt, Washington, and Jefferson). No modern president ranks in the Near Great category (T. Roosevelt, Wilson, Jackson, and Truman). Three rank in the Above Average category (L. Johnson at number 10, with Eisenhower and Kennedy at numbers 11 and 13, respectively). Two modern presidents are listed near the bottom of the Average category (Ford at number 24 and Carter at 25). One rates in the Below Average category (Reagan at 28). And one stands as a Failure (Nixon at number 35 of 37 presidents). See Table 1.3 for a list of all the presidents through Reagan.

Thus, the average rating of the presidents under study would be 24.4, placing the composite near the bottom of the Average category. If Johnson is removed and we consider only presidents Nixon to Reagan, the average plummets to a dismal 28, the Below Average category. Such ratings do not inspire admiration. (See Figure 1.2 for ratings of all presidents over time.)

✪ GOVERNING A LEAKY SHIP

Is the modern period unique? Was there at one time, a magical period when great presidents abounded, when good presidents were numerous? Saying that the string of modern presidents performed poorly should not imply that there were extended periods of great leadership to which the recent years should be compared. True, there were times and conditions when individual presidents rose to greatness, overcame the constraints inherent in the office and governed successfully. But this is more the exception than the norm. If past is prelude, we should *expect* presidents to do poorly. Presidents are today in much the same position their presidential forefathers have been in: a fairly limited state of power, a fairly wide array of restraints. While there are differences between the modern and traditional periods of the presidency—the role of television, the propensity for presidents to "go public," the United States as a superpower, the rise of the national security state—there are also a number of historical continuities that stand out,[52] the most pronounced of which is the institutional design of the separation (and sharing) of power. Thus, the failure of leadership in the United States is not a phenomenon peculiar to the modern period. All presidents face enormous constraints, and most presidents are unable to overcome the multiple roadblocks built into the presidential condition.

Cries of "crisis" are not new. But there is an added urgency in the modern period. In the nineteenth century, presidential ineffectiveness and governmental gridlock *were* problems, but they were problems restricted primarily to the United States and its future. Today, with the end of the Cold War and with the

Table 1.3 RATING THE U.S. PRESIDENTS: Murray and Blessing Poll

GREAT	NEAR GREAT	ABOVE AVERAGE
Abraham Lincoln	Theodore Roosevelt	John Adams
Franklin D. Roosevelt	Woodrow Wilson	Lyndon B. Johnson
George Washington	Andrew Jackson	Dwight D. Eisenhower
Thomas Jefferson	Harry S Truman	James K. Polk
		John Kennedy
		James Madison
		James Monroe
		John Quincy Adams
		Grover Cleveland

AVERAGE	BELOW AVERAGE	FAILURE
William McKinley	Zachary Taylor	Andrew Johnson
William Taft	Ronald Reagan	James Buchanan
Martin Van Buren	John Tyler	Richard Nixon
Herbert Hoover	Millard Fillmore	Ulysses S. Grant
Rutherford B. Hayes	Calvin Coolidge	Warren G. Harding
Chester A. Arthur	Franklin Pierce	
Gerald Ford		
Jimmy Carter		
Benjamin Harrison		

United States as the world's only remaining superpower, the failure of U.S. leadership, both at home and abroad, can have dramatic (and possibly tragic) consequences. Scholars and practitioners (from Alexander Hamilton to Woodrow Wilson to Thomas Cronin) have been concerned about the dispersion of political power and the recurrent problem associated with giving direction to a fragmented government. The persistence or recurrence of crises in presidential leadership can be attributed to a variety of factors (which are discussed in Chapter 2), but it is clear that institutionally the presidency is a troubled and troubling office. From its inception the presidency has confused and confounded those who wished to give energy to government while also maintaining democratic controls on officeholders. Confusion has reigned supreme because for the past two hundred years, we have never been certain what we

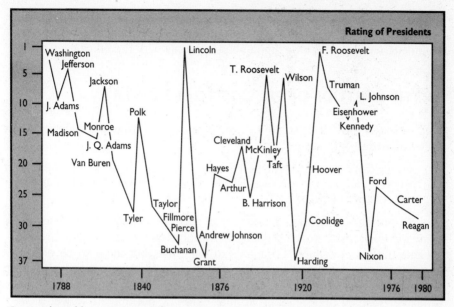

Source: Adapted from Murray and Blessing data, in Richard Rose, *The Postmodern President* (2 ed., Chatham, N.J.: Chatham House Publishers, 1991, p. 285).

Figure 1.2 Historians Rate U.S. Presidents.

really want of our president: powerful king or servant of the people, repository of government authority or constrained administrator. As Jimmy Breslin has noted, "The Office of President is such a bastardized thing, half royalty and half democracy, that nobody knows whether to genuflect or spit."[53]

The office of the presidency has an enormous, larger-than-life quality. In spite of the dramatic ups and downs of the office in the past fifty years, it does seem to be, in Arthur Schlesinger's words, "the indestructible" institution.[54] It is at once the most powerful *and* weakest executive office in the world. The great opportunity to do good is matched by the equally strong capacity to do great harm. The constitutional design of the office was left vague enough to give presidents an opportunity to shape and mold the office to conform—in part—to the needs of the time, the level of political opportunity, and the skills of each incumbent. But it was also an office encumbered by obstacle after obstacle. As political scientist James David Barber reminds us:

> But the Presidency is much more than an institution. It is a focus of feelings. . . . The Presidency is the focus for the most intense and persistent emotions in the American polity. the President is a symbolic leader, the one figure who draws to- gether the people's hopes and fears for the political future. On top of all his rou- tine duties he has to carry that off—or fail.[55]

But if there were Washingtons, Jeffersons, Jacksons, Lincolns, and Roosevelts who stamped their imprints on the office, there were also—and more commonly—Buchanans, Grants, Hardings, Pierces, Coolidges, Fillmores, and Tylers, who were overwhelmed and defeated by the office. In fact, the office ends up defeating most presidents. When failures far outnumber successes, it is time to ask: Is something fundamentally wrong with the office itself?

✪ THE FINITUDE OF PRESIDENTIAL POWER

Peter Drucker presents a straightforward way of answering this question. "The rule," he writes, "is simple":

> Any job that has defeated two or three men in succession, even though each had performed well in his previous assignments, must be assumed unfit for human beings. It must be redesigned.[56]

By Drucker's measure, the American presidency must be considered a "dysfunctional institution." To those who would argue that, "Yes, the presidency gets the better of most occupants of the office, but there *are* several successes," I would caution you to remember that *most* of the great and near great presidents arose in times of crisis, times when the normal checks and balances which so frustrate presidents in "normal" times do not operate very effectively (e.g., Lincoln, FDR). It is precisely this failure of presidential leadership (along with other factors, of course) that helps to create crisis situations, which then centralize power and allow presidents to exercise leadership away from the constraints of the checks-and-balances straitjacket.

If presidents usually fail but sometimes succeed, we must try to understand under what conditions, with which skills, at which times, presidents are more or less likely to be successful. What factors lead to presidential success or failure? Why do so many leaders fail to govern well in the American political system? Why did each of the past four presidents produce such a paltry record? Having established the relative ineffectiveness of the modern presidents, we can now turn our attention to the reasons why presidents so often fail.

✪ FOR DISCUSSION

1. The author attempts to make the case that the presidency, at least in the past twenty-five years, has "failed," that it has not lived up to our expectations or to the standards one may apply to a functional system of governance. Has the presidency really failed? Is the author being too harsh? Are you satisfied with the president's performance? Do you disagree with the author's conclusions about the modern presidency?

2. Are our expectations for the presidency too high? Are we being unrealistic in our hopes for presidential leadership?

3. Which president(s) do you like? Why? What is it about that president that makes him stand out in your eyes?

4. Growing up, what do you recall as your first memories of "the government"? Of the presidency?

✪ DEBATE QUESTIONS

Divide the class up into small (3 or 4 people) debate groups, and use one class period to conduct a debate on one of the following questions:

  I. Resolved: That the modern presidents should be considered failures.
 II. Resolved: That questions of personal character and private behavior have no place in the presidential selection process.

Chapter 2

★★

AMERICA'S LEADERSHIP AVERSION SYSTEM

It is no accident that in the United States, leaders usually can't lead. Presidents are often mere officeholders and only rarely leaders. In effect the deck is stacked against presidential leadership. The presidency is dealt a very weak power hand. How each president plays the hand he is dealt, how he uses his skills and opportunities, goes a long way in determining the success or failure of his administration. But *skill is not enough*. A variety of built-in roadblocks create an immunity system against leadership in all but the most extraordinary of times (i.e., crisis).

The power resources at a president's disposal, the ponderous and debilitating process of decision making, the obstructionist tendencies of the system, the demand overload, and a host of other impediments make it especially difficult to galvanize the machinery of government into action. In terms of power resources, the presidency is rather anemic, and many initiatives get swallowed into the black hole of presidential weakness. And yet, the public expects, even *demands* that the president provide direction for the government. However, while demands are high, the powers to meet these expectations are very limited. Everywhere he turns (with the notable exceptions of crises and some areas of foreign policy), the president faces an array of obstacles in his path. If a president is to succeed, he must somehow find a way either to gain collaboration from the other elements of the separated government or else to try to impose his will on this system.

In the United States, the gap between expectations and resources, image and reality of power, is enormous. In effect, there is a huge gap between what is expected of a president and what he can realistically deliver. As a focus of national attention, the presidency truly is, in John Kennedy's words, the "vital center" of American government. But in *power* terms (the ability to get people to do something they wouldn't otherwise do), the presidency is only a *part* of an interconnected system of government; a part that must *share power* with other actors in the system.

This creates what Heclo and Salamon call "the illusion of presidential government." As Heclo writes, "Presidential government is an illusion—an illusion that misleads presidents no less than the media and the American public, an illusion that often brings about the destruction of the very men who hold the office."[57] Encasing the president is a web of restraints, a network of checks, which bind presidents and limit their power. Lyndon Johnson expressed the frustrations of office to his successor Richard Nixon thus:

> Before you get to be president you think you can do anything. You think you're the most powerful leader since God. But when you get in that tall chair, as you're gonna find out, Mr. President, you can't count on people. You'll find your hands tied and people cussin' you. The office is kinda like the little country boy who found the hoochie-koochie show at the carnival, once he'd paid his dime and got inside the tent: "It ain't exactly as it was advertised."[58]

Is the institution that seems so power*ful* really so power*less*? In some ways, yes. There are a number of obstacles that prevent presidents from being effective leaders. It should thus not be surprising that *most* presidents perform poorly most of the time. But why? What variables inhibit presidential performance? The nine major factors that work against presidential power and effectiveness are: (1) the Intent of the Framers; (2) the Structure of American Government; (3) the Individual Skills of presidents; (4) America's Political Culture; (5) the Moods and Cycles of American Politics; (6) the Decline of Intermediaries; (7) Presidential Selection; (8) the "Market as Prison"; and (9) the Politics of Decline. These nine factors can be reduced to three clusters of variables: *external* (1, Intent of the Framers; 4, Political Culture; 5, Moods/Cycles; 8, Market as Prison; and 9, Politics of Decline); *process* (2, Structure of Government; 6, Decline of Intermediaries; and 7, Presidential Selection); and *individual* (3, Individual Skills of presidents).

These are the main barriers to presidential effectiveness, comprising an anti-leadership or leadership aversion system. They form the presidential fault-line that can suddenly snap and leave the president buried in the earthquake. We now turn to an analysis of the elements along this fault line.

✪ THE INTENT OF THE FRAMERS

The Framers of the United States Constitution created—by design—an "anti-leadership" system of government. While on the surface this may sound bizarre, upon reflection, it is clear that their primary goal—rather than to provide for an especially efficient system—was to create a government that would not jeopardize liberty. Freedom was their goal; governmental power their nemesis. Thus the men who toiled on that hot summer of 1787 in Philadelphia created an executive institution, a presidency, which had *limited powers*.

'Okay, bring in the new guy ...'

Reprinted by permission: *Philadelphia Inquirer.*

Essentially, the Framers wanted to counteract two fears: the fear of the *mob* (democracy, or mobocracy) and the fear of the *monarchy* (centralized, tyrannical executive power). In fact, the menacing image of England's King George III— against whom the colonists rebelled and whom Thomas Paine called "the Royal Brute of Britain"—served the Framers as a powerful reminder of the dangers of a strong executive. Thus, to contain power, they set up an executive office that was constitutionally rather *weak* (Congress had—on paper at least— most of the power), dependent on the *rule of law*, with a *separation of powers* in order to ensure a system of *checks and balances*.

For James Madison, the chief architect of the Constitution, a government with too much power was a dangerous government. Seeing himself as a keen student of history, he believed that *human nature* drove men—at this time, only men were allowed to enter the public arena—to pursue *self-interest*, and therefore a system of government designed to have "ambition checked by ambition" set within rather strict limits was the only hope to establish a stable government that did not endanger liberty. Realizing that "enlightened statesmen" would not always guide the nation, Madison embraced a check-and-balance system of separate but overlapping and shared powers. Madison's concern to have a government with controlled and limited powers is seen throughout his writings, but nowhere is it more vivid than when he wrote in *Federalist* 51, "You must first enable the government to control the governed; and in the next place, oblige it to control itself."[59]

Yes, government had to have enough power to govern, but no, it couldn't have enough power to overwhelm liberty. If one branch could check another, tyranny might be thwarted. In Madison's writings there is scant concern expressed for the needs of a *strong* government. Thus, the Constitution became both an enabling *and* a disabling document.

As the great defender of a strong executive, Alexander Hamilton emerged. An advocate of strong central government, Hamilton promoted, especially in the *Federalist Papers*, a version of executive power quite different from Madison's dispersed and separate powers. Where Madison wanted to check authority, Hamilton wished to support it; where Madison believed that the new government's powers should be "few and defined," Hamilton wanted to infuse the executive with "energy."[60] Hamilton advocated vigorous government and a strong presidency. As Hamilton wrote in *Federalist* 70, good government requires "energy," and he scornfully rejected the weak executive:

> A feeble executive implies a feeble execution of the government. A feeble execution is but another phrase for a bad execution; and a government ill executed, whatever it may be in theory, must be, in practice, a bad government.

Hamilton sought a strong president within a more centralized government. But such a system would undermine Madison's determination to check government power. The presidency, a unitary office headed by one man, would have no *internal* check. Thus, to Madison, there was the need for strong *external* checks, that is, a strong Congress. While Madison may have won the day at the Constitutional Convention, creating a presidency with fairly limited powers, history has been on the side of Hamilton, as the presidency has grown to resemble the Hamiltonian model more than was originally intended by the Framers.

Always looming in the background—quite literally, as he was in France at the time of the Philadelphia Constitutional Convention—was the enormous presence of Thomas Jefferson. An advocate of small government and democracy, Jefferson was very suspicious of power (his behavior as president aside). But Jefferson's vision of a decentralized government, an agrarian economy, and a robust democracy was given little attention at the Convention. It was a Madisonian model that emerged.

Madison, like most of the Founders, feared government in the hands of the people, but he likewise feared too much power in the hands of one man. Therefore, the Madisonian model called both for protections against mass democracy *and* limits on governmental power. This is not to say that the Founders wanted a weak and ineffective government; had that been their goal, they could have kept the Articles of Confederation. But they did want a government that could not too easily act. The theory of government that the Madisonian design necessitates is one of consensus, coalition, and cooperation—on the one hand—and checks, vetoes, and balances on the other.

A rough balance was sought between governmental power and individual liberty. The government had to be strong enough to act but restrained enough so as not to threaten liberty. By separating powers, forcing institutions to share powers, and limiting powers via the rule of law, the Founders hoped both to allow power (ambition) to counter power and to decrease the opportunity for powers to be abused. Since the people could not be trusted to govern, and since as Madison wrote in *Federalist* 10, "Enlightened statesmen will not always be at the helm," power had to be fragmented and dispersed.

The result was that when left strictly to its own devices, the presidency is a rather weak institution. The dilemma thus created—especially in the modern period—is how can a president bring Hamiltonian energy, to this Madisonian system, for Jeffersonian ends! The Framers did not make it easy for the government to act or for presidents to lead—that was decidedly not their intent—and they left the powers and contours of the office somewhat vague, expecting George Washington to fill in the gaps. This created, in Edward S. Corwin's words, "an invitation to struggle" for control of government.[61] Looking at the Framers design for government, a modern efficiency expert would likely conclude that the system could not work very well: too many limits, too many checks; not enough power, not enough leadership. But that is the way the Framers wanted it.

✪ THE STRUCTURE OF AMERICAN GOVERNMENT

What exactly did the Framers create? What structure or skeleton of power and government did the Founders of the U.S. system design? The chief mechanisms that they established to control as well as to empower the executive (mentioned briefly in the previous section) are as follows: (1) *Limited Government*, a reaction against the arbitrary, expansive powers of the king or state, and a protection of personal liberty; (2) *Rule of Law*, so that only on the basis of legal or constitutional grounds could the government act; (3) *Separation of Powers*, so that the three branches of government each would have a defined sphere of power; and (4) *Checks and Balances*, so that each branch could limit or control the powers of the other branches of government.

In this structure, what *powers* and *resources* has the president? Limited powers. Constitutionally, the United States faces a paradox: the Constitution both *empowers* and *restrains* government. In fact, the Constitution does not clearly spell out the power of the presidency. Article 1 is devoted to the Congress, the first and constitutionally the most powerful branch of government. Article 2, the executive article, deals with the presidency. The president's power cupboard is—compared to that of the Congress—nearly bare. Section 1 gives the "executive power" to the president but does not reveal whether this is a grant of tangible power or merely a title. Section 2 makes the president commander in chief of the armed forces but reserves the power to *declare* war for the Congress. Section 2 also gives the president absolute power to grant reprieves and pardons, power to make treaties (with the advice and consent of the Senate), and the power to nominate ambassadors, judges, and other public ministers (with the advice and consent of the Senate). Section 3 calls for the president to inform the Congress on the state of the Union and to recommend measures to Congress; grants the power to receive ambassadors; and imposes upon the president the duty to see that the laws are faithfully executed. These powers are significant, but in and of themselves they do not suggest a very strong or independent institution, and certainly not a national leadership position.

The Framers were clearly pulled in two different directions when inventing the president.[62] They wanted to give the executive enough "energy" to act and yet not enough to endanger liberty or promote tyranny. But, as political scientist Lyn Ragsdale notes, "Energy and safety are contradictory requirements."[63]

Thus, the president has two types of power: *formal*, the ability to command, and *informal*, the ability to persuade. The president's formal powers are limited and (often) shared. The president's informal powers are a function of skill, situation, and political time (there is more about the president's power in Chapter 3). While the formal power of the president remains fairly constant over time, the president's informal powers are quite variable, dependent on the skill of each individual president. This is not to suggest that the president's formal powers are static—over time, presidential power has increased significantly—but the pace of change has been such that it was well over a hundred years before the presidency assumed primacy in the U.S. political system.

How much power does the president possess? Who governs in America? Bert Rockman adresses this question when he writes:

> Precisely where does this situate the presidency? The president is, after all, not the leader of "a government" but a leader who heads only a part of government—a chief of state in a society whose culture resists the idea (but *only* the idea) of the state. The American form of government handicaps ambition in the White House, and presidential success in accomplishing objectives hinges upon support generated across other institutions. . . . The power to govern could never be assumed. It would always have to be struggled for in an environment of interdependence—the direct result of Madison's triumph, and the indirect result of Jefferson's conquest of the American political spirit.[64]

The president has few independent powers, many shared powers. Most are shared with a Congress that has greater enumerated constitutional powers (see Article 1) but less of an institutional capacity to act. Sharing powers with a Congress that only occasionally responds to presidential initiatives makes leadership a hazardous minefield.

The constitutional structure of the government *disperses* or *fragments* power: with no recognized, authoritative vital center, power is fluid and floating; no one branch can very easily or freely act without the consent (formal or tacit) of another branch. Power was designed to counteract power; ambition to check ambition. This structure was developed by men whose memories of tyranny and the arbitrary exercise of power by the king of England was fresh in their minds. It was a structure designed to force a *consensus* before the government could act. The structure of government created by the Framers did not create *a* leadership institution, but several—three separate, semiautonomous institutions that shared power. As James Pfiffner notes, "The Framers designed a system of shared powers within a system that is purposefully biased against change."[65] The forces of the status quo were given multiple veto opportunities; the forces of change were forced to go into battle nearly unarmed.

Because there are so many potential veto points, the American system generally alternates between stasis and crisis, paralysis and spasm. On occasion, the branches are able to cooperate and work together to promote change, but it is especially difficult for the president and Congress—deliberately disconnected by the Framers—to forge a union. The resulting paralysis has many parents, but the separation of powers is clearly the most determinative.

The Framers purposely created uncertainty about who holds power in the United States. A system of baroque cross-powers and checked powers created a constitutional mechanism that prohibits one branch from exercising too much power on its own. Opportunities to check power abound; opportunities to exercise power are limited. As political scientist Bert Rockman reminds us,

> The architect designed many doors, each seemingly with a different lock. In normal times there would be more locks than keys. Without the intervention of war (and, since Korea, even then) or the appearance of crisis, or the preponderance of like-minded majorities, the independence of institutions so greatly valued by Madison is conducive to the grinding, rather than the meshing, of gears. . . . What emerges is not "a government," but many, often competitive and sometimes cooperative, governments; not a decisive point of decision making at the center, but a diffusion

of decisional points; and not a state presumably representing a "common and durable interest," but a society whose abundant pluralism finds ready expression through the many conduits available in the polity.[66]

Again, this system of separation of powers was designed to thwart tyranny, not to promote efficiency. By its own standards, it has worked quite well. But the natural lethargy built into the system now threatens to grind it to a halt. The failure of government to govern, to act, to solve problems, now seems so overpowering that the fundamental legitimacy of the system is increasingly threatened.

Presidential leadership of Congress is further complicated by the persistence of divided government, in which, often, one party controls the White House while another party controls the Congress. As if presidents needed more reason to feel frustrated, the modern period has been one of divided government, with the "Republicanization of the presidency" and the "Democratization of the Congress." It is no accident that, from 1968 to 1992, the persistence of divided government (the Carter presidency being the exception: 1976–80) has corresponded with periods of failed leadership.[67] Divided government makes the already fragmented system of government divisive, and thus it is less likely to produce the cohesion and cooperation necessary for the branches to work together.

This fluidity and fragmentation of power creates a situation in which "the government" is controlled not by any single person or place but by different people in different places (if it exists at all). Rockman notes that while there is, in a technical sense, "a government,"

> there is no unified government, no government of the day in the modern sense of that term. Instead, the design of the separation of powers system is predicated on the view expressed by Madison in *Federalist* 51 that such a system is essential for the maintenance of liberty. . . . The result is a government founded on defensiveness. Each of its parts can be assertive, but the assertiveness of the parts makes for an unassertiveness of the whole. . . . In short the system of separated powers was (and largely remains) an institutional design meant to frustrate the exercise of power. This is so because American institutions do not so much divide *powers* as they divide *power*. In Samuel Huntington's well-turned sentence, "America perpetuated a fusion of functions and a division of power, while Europe developed a differentiation of functions and a centralization of power." Clearly, whatever the virtues of these antique institutions, their strong suit is not the efficient direction of an active government.[68]

The structure of government is thus stacked against presidential leadership. The result is that in all but the most unusual of circumstances, *institutional impotence* characterizes the American presidency. The amazing thing, then, is not that presidents usually fail—that is built into the very structure of American government—but that presidents sometimes succeed! (See Chapter 3.) With so much working against them, it should not surprise us when presidents stumble and fall.

✪ INDIVIDUAL SKILLS

A number of presidential scholars argue that "if we could only get the *right person* in the White House, most of our problems would evaporate." Historian Arthur Schlesinger, Jr., challenges the structuralists, who argue that the separation of powers inhibits strong leadership, and insists that *skilled presidents* have been able to overcome structural roadblocks. He writes:

> Is the difficulty we encounter these days in meeting our problems really the consequence of defects in the structure of our government? After all, we have had the separation of powers from the beginning of the republic. This has not prevented competent presidents from acting with decision and dispatch. The separation of powers did not notably disable Jefferson or Jackson or Lincoln or Wilson or the Roosevelts. . . . The real difference is that the presidents who operated the system successfully knew what they thought should be done—and were able to persuade

Congress and the nation to give their remedies a try. . . . Our problem is not at all
that we know what to do and are impeded from doing it by some structural logjam
in the system. Our problem—let us face it—is that we do not know what to do.[69]

While there is some merit to this argument—yes, skill does matter—it only
tackles part of the problem of failed leadership. Skill is of great importance, but
it is not enough. Getting better leaders would help, but it would not solve the
leadership void in American government.

One would be hard-pressed to defend the job performance of individuals
who have served as presidents in the modern period. As Chapter 1 of this
work suggests, the United States has had, for a quarter century, a series of
presidents who simply were not up to the task of governing. Johnson, with
flawed character; Nixon, with deeply flawed character; Ford, decent but inept;
Carter, decent but politically naive; Reagan, the amiable dunce; and Bush,
the visionless manager—all seemed to wrest political defeat from the jaws of
victory.

The Search for a Savior as president overemphasizes the personal and
underemphasizes the institutional. Much more is at work here than skill. As
this study indicates, more is at fault than individual failings—as significant
as they may be. True, recent presidents have not been an especially distin-
guished lot, but the fault is only partially theirs. Skilled leaders *could have*
done better, but even with a greater reservoir of skill, there are roadblocks
and hurdles that all presidents face, which make it very difficult to lead. When
one combines limited skill with these other inhibitors, the result is failed
leadership.

Presidential scholars agree that skill is important, but how important?
Under what circumstances? No scholar is more identified with the skill argument than Richard Neustadt. His 1960 book *Presidential Power*[70] is still considered one of the most important and useful books ever written about presidential politics. Neustadt recognizes that the system or structure of the American
system is designed to frustrate presidential leadership, and he argues that to
overcome these roadblocks, presidents must make optimal use of their *informal*
power resources: skill, prestige, reputation. Only then can presidents solve the
"power problem" of the American system of government.

To have any hope of being successful in an anti-leadership system, presidents must employ a vast repertoire of skills and experiences: managerial skill,
political skill, political experience, personal style, psychological traits, and so
forth. Not all presidents have all the skills necessary to overcome the systemic
roadblocks they face, but wise presidents who lack skills *can* use their staffs and
cabinet to compensate (there is more on the use of skill in Chapter 3).

If the presidency requires a leader with the skill level of an FDR, a crisis
such as the Great Depression, and a huge legislative majority in order to govern, then the institution itself is deeply flawed. Even FDR, the very model of
presidential skill, needed a crisis and vast congressional majority to lead. But
not all presidents are FDR, and of late, the American voter seems intent on

electing inexperienced outsiders to the White House (with damaging consequences). Three of the past four presidents had *no* Washington, D.C., experience, nor did they have any foreign policy experience. Is it any wonder that recent presidents have made a tough job all that much more difficult?

✪ AMERICA'S POLITICAL CULTURE

Are the citizens of the United States culturally inclined toward good citizenship/followership? The answer to this question is very much a mixed bag. What does it take to be a good citizen/follower?

The emergence of leaders within a group is both inevitable and necessary. However, leadership is but one side of the coin. For, if we are to have good leadership, we must also have good followership. Leadership matters, but what is leadership without followership? The general would be nothing without well-trained troops; the plant manager would be incapacitated without good workers; and, yes, the college president would be nothing without a highly professional faculty. As James M. Burns notes, "Great leaders require great followers."[71]

But, what do we mean by followers? Lemmings following the leader off the cliff? Obedient, submissive, order-following conformists? Hardly. John Gardner notes that twentieth-century institutions have been caught in a savage cross fire between "uncritical lovers and unloving critics." Gardner goes on to remind us that love without criticism brings stagnation, and criticism without love brings destruction.[72] Today, as public outrage alternates with disgust and apathy, what can we expect of citizens?

What, then, do we mean when we refer to good followership? There are five key tasks in followership: (1) *commitment*: support for the goals and values of the community; (2) *idea generation*: creative problem-solving and the percolation of ideas and pressure up to the top (what Tom Cronin calls Act 1 leadership); (3) *competence*: a degree of professionalism and skill; (4) *informed criticism*: knowledge matched with the ability to disagree agreeably; and (5) *self-management*: self-reliance, independence, and self-control.

How do leadership and followership fit together? What is needed? Equally—in government, business and the workplace, the university and the community—we need a shared commitment and shared responsibility to the shared destiny of the organization: a sense of *community*. Leadership is a collective enterprise, as is followership. Both must focus on developing a sense in which all rise and fall together.

Culturally, does the United States foster values and attitudes that promote a healthy sense of followership/citizenship for a democratic political system? By *culture* we mean those ideas and values, norms and symbols that comprise the American identity. The key components of America's political culture include a commitment to *democracy* (an open, egalitarian political system); *liberty* (get or keep the government off my back); and a *competitive* culture (which often sets citizen off against citizen) in a *capitalist* economic system (which is competitive) with an emphasis on *materialism* (in which accumulation and consumption loom large). These prevailing attitudes are set within a *legalistic* framework (which is adversarial in nature) with a strong commitment to the *Judeo-Christian* ethos (Americans have a comparatively high identification with organized religions) in a culture of *individualism* (in which the self is elevated over the group). The combination of these factors comprises what is often referred to as the American Creed, which is essentially antigovernment and antiauthority in nature. The governing ethos in America thus imposes a series of restraints on the exercise of leadership. Clinton Rossiter captures this dilemma when he writes:

> We have always been a nation obsessed with liberty. Liberty over authority, freedom over responsibility, rights over duties—these are our historic preferences. . . . Not the good man, but the free man has been the measure of all things in this 'sweet land of liberty'; not national glory, but individual liberty has been the object of political authority and the test of its worth.[73]

The combinations of these conflicting values often pull the public in different directions and are sometimes quite contradictory. For example, the commitments to individualism, competitiveness, and materialism make the average citizen ambitious, result-oriented, and productive. These same attributes also make the average citizen highly independent. Further, they work to make most Americans resistant to authority, suspicious of community, reluctant to solve problems as a group. Thus, "politics" becomes a four-letter word, and followership becomes problematic: an anti-leadership culture.

How does this American Creed affect our attitudes toward leadership? While it creates a fundamentally anti-leadership disposition, the American propensity for individualism does generate a type of hero worship that feeds into the heroic model of the presidency. We thus honor the patriot Washington; the great democrats Jefferson and Jackson; the savior Lincoln; and the great one FDR. But such hero worship masks, in some ways, the stronger cultural pull, which is anti-leadership and antiauthority. As Thomas E. Cronin writes,

> The paradoxes of the presidency do not lie in the White House but in the emotings, feelings, and expectations of us all. There exists some element in the American mind, and perhaps in the minds of people everywhere, that it is possible to find a savior-hero who will deliver us to an era of greener grass and a land of milk and honey. When this pseudomessiah fails we inflict upon him the wrath of our vengeance. It is almost a ritual destruction; we venerate the presidency, but we destroy our presidents.[74]

In general, it is the antiauthority strain of the American Creed that has dominated in our culture. Max Lerner has written that "American thinkers have been at their best in their antiauthoritarianism."[75] From Jefferson and Madison to Calhoun and Thoreau, some of America's most profound and influential thinkers reflected deep strains of individualism and antiauthoritarianism. The implications of this for leadership were not lost on that thoughtful French observer of the American scene Alexis de Tocqueville:

> When it comes to the influence of one man's mind over another's, that is necessarily very restricted in a country where the citizens have all become more or less similar . . . and since they do not recognize any signs of incontestable greatness or superiority in any of their fellows, are continually brought back to their own judgment as the most apparent and accessible test of truth. So it is not only confidence in any particular man which is destroyed. There is a general distaste for accepting any man's word as proof of anything.[76]

It is very difficult (except in a crisis) for presidents to ask the people to make sacrifices for the common good, to move beyond self-interest. When Jimmy Carter asked citizens to turn their thermostats down to 68°F (20°C) during the oil crisis, he was scorned. It should not be a surprise that when he ran for reelection he lost to a candidate with a spend-spend, buy-buy philosophy.

The United States lacks a coherent *public philosophy* of the role and purpose of government. Americans have always been a bit ambivalent regarding power and government, suspicious of authority (which is in many ways quite healthy in a democracy, but it also makes governing quite difficult).

A major shortcoming of this lack of a public philosophy is the lack of consensus as to what *we* as a people should do, where *we* as a nation need to move. As French sociologist Michel Crozier has written, we have "the land of consensus turned into the land of disorder and tumult."[77]

The sense of a shared community, of a social contract, remains murky. We are not "one nation indivisible" but a collection of atomized individuals. Rarely do we pull together for the common good. Are we a "nation," a loose-knit collection of individuals, or a confederation of tribes?[78]

Effective leadership requires a supporting *consensus* behind governmental authority and presidential initiatives. Both are currently lacking. Disharmony and conflict characterize the American polity. A divided nation, a polarized nation, cannot be a well-governed nation. "Where did we go wrong?" asks leadership expert Warren Bennis. "America has always been at war with itself. We have always dreamt of community and democracy but always practiced individualism and capitalism. We have celebrated innocence but sought power. We are the world's leading sentimentalists, and it's a very short step from sentimentality to cynicism."[79]

While Americans demonstrate a high degree of patriotic fervor, they do not demonstrate a deep sense of *community*. From a strong commitment to community, one can elicit a *consensus* upon which to build *leadership*. Lacking a strong sense of community, leaders have a difficult time pulling the nation together (except in a crisis) to respond collectively, politically, as a nation. It is very hard to mobilize the people to pursue a public good. The major roadblock to building community is the powerful strain of *individualism* that dominates the attitudes of citizens of the United States. "We are a nation of Ones, and the political consequences are powerful."[80]

Samuel Huntington argues that American political culture is characterized by an "antipower ethic" dominated by belief in equality, liberty, individualism, and democracy, all of which are "antigovernment and antiauthority in character."[81] James Madison's vision—grounded in a pessimistic view of human nature—was that the problem of factions was "sown into the nature of man," and this necessitated limits and controls on power.[82] We could not be trusted to act together (democracy); we were too self-interested to be left entirely to our own devices. Thus was created a strictly limited government, which was designed to structure conflict, to set interest off against interest, and to embrace a strictly individualistic view. This view did not eliminate politics or collective action, but it did set as the premise of government, *individuals* acting out of their own self-interest, alone, not in concert. Thus, being a leader in the United States is somewhat akin to trying to herd cats.

❂ THE MOODS AND CYCLES OF AMERICAN POLITICS

Leadership does not occur in a time warp. There are different "seasons" of leadership, times when presidents are afforded more or less room for power.[83]

These cycles (some would call it a dialectic) take many forms: the business cycle of economic growth followed by recession; the political pendulum of liberalism followed by a conservative period; the mood swing of public confidence in government followed by a retreat into private interests and cynicism; the foreign policy shifts from isolationism to international involvement. These cycles are, for the most part, beyond the control of presidents, but they do have a great impact on presidential power. As Bert Rockman notes,

> The culture of American politics and the structure of American government each predispose against the prospects for achieving and then sustaining coherent direction. To be sure, the obstacles to achieving direction are not at all times equally severe. Opportunities for directive leadership ebb and flow, the product of cycles of longer and shorter duration. Within these cycles are phases during which some of the normal constraints on leadership are relaxed, and, of course, times during which these constraints become more inhibiting.[84]

There are times when (and conditions under which) presidents are afforded a great deal of leverage and power (e.g., a crisis). There are also times when presidents are kept on a fairly short leash (a weak economy, low presidential popularity, etc.).

For example, in the aftermath of the war in Vietnam and Watergate, the public turned against the government and presidential power and the United States entered a president-bashing mood. Presidents Ford and Carter were severely restricted in their opportunities to exercise power. The public was cynical and suspicious, the press was hostile, the Congress was reasserting its authority, and—if that weren't enough—the economy was in free fall. Even if Ford and Carter had been highly skilled, gifted politicians (which they were not), their level of political opportunity was so low that there is almost no way they could have been very successful.

By contrast, FDR, a highly skilled politician, also benefited from a level of opportunity that was unusually high. He came to office (1933) at a time when the public *demanded* strong leadership, when the Congress was willing to accede power to the president. Thus, the mixture of high skill and high opportunity granted FDR both power and success.

Political time is of importance.[85] During periods of regime change and social disruption, certain types of leadership will be more necessary, while during periods of normalcy, a different type of leadership may be required. Likewise, during periods of crisis,[86] a different sort of leadership is required. Clearly, there is not a leadership for all seasons. Effective leaders are able to adjust to these different seasons; they style-flex.

Several cycles are especially relevant to presidential leadership. One is the *succession cycle*. Valerie Bunce notes that major policy shifts are *most likely* when new leaders take over.[87] Thus, leadership change is the key to policy change. There is also the *cycle of decreasing popularity*. In general, over time, presidents lose popular support, making it more difficult to put together political coalitions as time progresses. Yet another presidential cycle is the *cycle of growing effectiveness*.[88] The presidential *learning curve* is at its lowest at the beginning of a president's term and rises as time goes by. Thus, presidents know more and more as time goes by. But their power is usually at its peak early in their terms, just when their knowledge is lowest. When presidents have the most power, they usually have the least knowledge.

In a broader sense, the cycle that seems most relevant to presidential leadership is the long-term ebb and flow, or pulse rate, of American politics. Historian Arthur M. Schlesinger, Jr., suggests that this cycle is like a pendulum swinging back and forth. The United States alternates between periods of "conservatism versus innovation" (Emerson); "diffusion versus centralization" (Henry Adams); "conservatism versus liberalism" (Arthur Schlesinger, Jr.); "divergent goals of public and private happiness" (Albert O. Hirskman); or "capitalism and democracy" (McCloosKy and Zaller). Schlesinger describes these mood swings or cycles as "a continuing shift in national involvement, between *public purpose* and *private interest*."[89]

Schlesinger argues that the roots of this repeating cycle lie deep in human nature and the U.S. structure of government, and the pattern follows a life cycle of a thirty-year alternation between the pursuit of public purpose and private interest. In the twentieth century, there have been three periods of high governmental activity in support of public purpose: Theodore Roosevelt in 1901, Franklin D. Roosevelt in 1933, and John F. Kennedy in 1961. There have also been "high tides of conservative restoration—the 1920s, the 1950s, the 1980s."[90]

Thus, the pulse of political change beats to an alternating, thirty-year pattern of high public purpose followed by high private interest. Erwin C. Hargrove adds to our understanding of leadership's impact on political change by focusing attention on the "cycles of the rise and fall of reform politics."[91] Hargrove sees a three-stage cycle of political reform: (1) "a period of preparation"; (2) "a burst of activism and reform"; and (3) "a time of reaction against the previous stage and therefore of consolidation and conservation."[92] Hargrove's three

Table 2.1 TWENTIETH-CENTURY PRESIDENTIAL CYCLES[93]

1 Preparation	2 Achievement of Reform	3 Consolidation
Theodore Roosevelt William Howard Taft	Woodrow Wilson	Warren Harding Calvin Coollidge Herbert Hoover
(Depression)	Franklin Roosevelt Harry Truman	Dwight Eisenhower
John F. Kennedy	Lyndon Johnson	Richard Nixon

stages (Table 2.1) fit neatly into Schlesinger's cycles of change, giving a more coherent framework to the role of presidential leadership in these change cycles.

There is a certain logic to this pace of political activity. Rather than running at a steady pace, political change in the United States resembles a sprinter more than a distance runner. There is a short, quick burst of activity (Hargrove's stage 2), followed by a much needed rest (stage 3), at which time the reforms of the period of accelerated activism are consolidated into the system, and the public has a chance to rest and recharge its batteries. But old problems persist, new ones emerge, and before long, there is a demand for change (stage 1). This leads to another burst of activity (stage 2), and the cycle repeats.

Thomas E. Cronin gives us a deeper insight into the connection between points in the cycle of change and the various types of leadership that are appropriate for different times and situations. Cronin sees leadership as evolving in three stages or acts, depending on the point in political time. These "acts" correspond to the Schlesinger and Hargrove cycles. In Act 1 (Hargrove's period of consolidation), since the public mood is more focused on private interest than public purpose (to use Schlesinger's terminology), "leaders are dreamers, visionaries, or creative catalysts."[94] In this stage, the down period of public activism, the "leader" is the (not so) average citizen who pushes, prods, creates new programs. Those to whom we conventionally look for leadership—officeholders—act as cautious consolidators, not creative risk-takers. Therefore, the responsibility to lead rests on the shoulders of the public.

Act 2 (Hargrove's period of preparation) finds an increased level of activity, but officeholders still display caution. As Cronin writes, "Act 2 leaders understand that no truly bold measure begins at the top. . . . Act 2 leaders will-

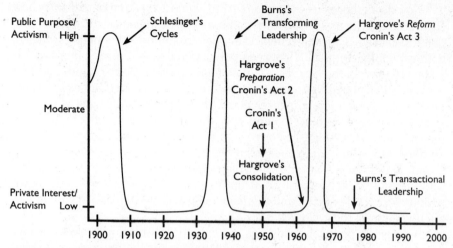

Figure 2.1 Leadership, Citizenship, and Political Change.

ingly enlarge and amplify conflict. . . ."[95] Here, the public agenda shifts to a recognition of public problems and the public begins to demand a governmental response.

By the time the cycle shifts to Hargrove's reform period, officeholders become more active, the public demands reform, and in Act 3, the "mainstream establishment" embraces political change, and officeholders actively pursue a reform agenda. This is the height of Schlesinger's period of public purpose.

Cronin's work shifts attention away from the officeholder as leader to the citizen as leader, what might be called a "shared leadership model." By recognizing the important role played by the public in political leadership, and by discriminating between the different types of leadership in operation at different times in the political cycle of change, Cronin broadens our understanding of the connection between leadership, citizenship, political change, and political time.

Finally, James M. Burns provides us with the final piece of our puzzle of leadership, citizenship, and political change with his distinction between *transactional* and *transforming* leadership.[96] Burns sees transactional leadership as an exchange, bargaining model. It is incremental in scope and narrow in range. Transforming leadership is more inspirational and nonincremental. It links leader and citizen together. This leadership taps something deep and fundamental in the people and is able to transform the political system. Transactional leadership generally corresponds to Schlesinger's down cycle, Hargrove's stage 1. Transforming leadership usually corresponds to the up stage of the cycle, Hargrove's achievement of reform. In the down period, a political leader's window of opportunity to act is fairly narrow. Thus transactional leadership usually fits this time frame. In an up cycle, the window of opportunity is fairly wide and the possibility of achieving transformational leadership exists.

How do all these pieces fit together? In Figure 2.1, I attempt to display how each scholar's ideas fit into this framework of leadership, citizenship, and political change. Schlesinger depicts a roller-coaster ride of dramatic swings in political reform, with shifts between public purpose and private interests. By adding Hargrove's three cycles, a certain logic emerges. Down periods allow for consolidation, absorption, conservation; the system can rest. But as problems build, preparation for reform takes place. Then, in a dramatic burst of political energy, reforms are achieved. Burns sees this shift as the distinction between transactional leadership (the down cycle, a period of consolidation) and transforming leadership (sometimes achieved in the up cycle, a time of reform). Cronin draws our attention to the role played by the public in these cycles, with Cronin identifying the "leadership" role played by "followers" in the down period of the cycle (Act 1) and the leadership role played by officeholders in the up period of the cycle (Act 3).

By viewing political change as a symbiotic connection between leader (officeholder) and follower (citizen) at different points in time, we can broaden our horizons to the complex and interconnected nature of political change in a democracy. Leaders don't always lead; followers don't always follow. Different points in political time require different types of political leadership and a different set of political skills.

✪ THE DECLINE OF INTERMEDIARIES

To move the machinery of government, presidents need help. They can only rarely act alone. Thus, presidents need mechanisms to grease the governmental wheels.

In the past, presidents have occasionally been able to rely on such things as a *consensus* among leaders and the public regarding the direction in which the nation should go, or relying on *strong congressional leaders* to move the president's program. At other times, presidents have been able to rely on *party support* to help get legislation through Congress. But consensus has degenerated into dissensus, congressional leadership has been disarmed, and the party system in the United States is relatively weak and nonideological (especially when compared with European counterparts). In recent years, the parties have further weakened, stripping presidents of a traditional tool in the struggle for power.[97]

When there is a general agreement on where the nation should go and how it should get there, when there is a *consensus*, it becomes easier to lead the government into action. But rarely can presidents rely on a consensus. Sometimes presidents can help create a consensus by focusing attention on particular issues, but even that is a relatively rare occurrence.

If presidents can only rarely rely on a consensus to aid in governing, can they at least rely on *congressional leaders* to guide their programs through congress? Stories of Lyndon Johnson's calling a few congressional leaders into the Oval Office for a late night chat and a few drinks—followed by Johnson's getting the congressional leaders to "deliver the votes" on a key issue—may be apocryphal, but they point to the potential (if not the ideal) of a president being able to use congressional leaders as intermediaries.

Congressional leaders can create a linkage between the separated president and Congress. But even when the president has a Congress controlled by his own party, he cannot rely on the leadership to deliver votes. This is because the leaders do not control the votes of the members. Members of Congress are more independent and entrepreneurial than in past years. The dramatic changes in Congress during the 1970s and 1980s have opened up the process, made it less hierarchical, more democratic, and less amenable to leadership. Thus, presidents must work harder to get less from the Congress.

The political party *can*, at its best, focus on issues and public opinion, organize the masses, cue voters, offer candidates, develop programs, lend organization and unity to the dispersed power arena, and lubricate the machinery of government. And most social scientists continue to agree with James MacGregor Burns's assertion that parties are "indispensable to democratic leadership."[98] Though Thomas Jefferson once noted, "If I could not go to heaven but with a party, I would not go there at all,"[99] in historical terms, parties have sometimes served as a great aid in a president's pursuit of policy goals.

But the modern parties, while making attempts to serve these functions, are often seen as weak and inadequate, unable to fulfill these roles. Political

Table 2.2 RECENT PRESIDENTIAL CANDIDATES

YEAR	DEMOCRAT	REPUBLICAN
1964	Lyndon B. Johnson	Barry Goldwater
1968	Hubert H. Humphrey	Richard M. Nixon
1972	George McGovern	Richard M. Nixon
1976	Jimmy Carter	Gerald Ford
1980	Jimmy Carter	Ronald Reagan
1984	Walter Mondale	Ronald Reagan
1988	Michael Dukakis	George Bush
1992	Bill Clinton	George Bush

parties have become much less important in developing the coalitions necessary to organize power and move government.[100] Instead of having reliable party coalitions from which to operate, presidents are forced to develop their own, ad hoc coalitions, using the media and "going public,"[101] directly addressing the people in a game of plebiscitary politics.[102] As the bond of party has proven inadequate to meet presidential needs, presidents have developed adapting strategies, primarily using the media but also acting on their own or acting in secret.

Thus, for presidents to govern, they must constantly campaign (a time-consuming and demanding task). To get elected, presidents must put together an *electoral coalition*, but to rule, presidents need a *governing coalition* (i.e., party support).[103] But without an adequate party system, presidents must perpetually "campaign," constantly play the popularity game, and always act like a candidate. This tends to trivialize politics and leaves precious little time for governing. In order to govern, presidents need help, and at various times in the past they could rely on intermediaries to provide it. Now they get less and less of this assistance and are thus left politically alone and vulnerable.

✪ PRESIDENTIAL SELECTION

In many ways, the U.S. presidential selection process is proof that Darwin was wrong! Could it really be argued that the "fittest" candidates are to be found in the list of recent choices for president? (See Table 2.2.)

James Burns calls the presidential selection process "the worst top leadership recruitment system in the democratic societies of the world."[104] Campaigns are *long*, lasting nearly three years (Rockman refers to it as the "endless campaign"), costly, media driven, gruelling, disruptive and intrusive on family life, trivial, overly personal, and often demeaning. Would anyone worthy of the office seek it?[105]

In the founding period, the nascent nation produced an array of leaders and statesmen of stunning quality: Washington, Jefferson, Madison, Hamilton, Franklin, Adams, and Paine, among others. In one generation, nearly a dozen truly outstanding men emerged. Today, the candidates seem like intellectual and moral dwarfs when compared to their forefathers. Is it that America has no great men or women left?

Rather than the assumption that the United States has no leaders capable of greatness, a more likely prospect is that the selection process tends to reward people with attributes that would generally be thought of as unwanted, and it tends to punish potential candidates who possess the qualities most desirable in a president.

Running for president is a three-year, full-time job. Shortly after the 1992 race ended, the 1996 presidential race began.[106] Who could, who would spend all that time running for president? Likewise, the need to attract campaign contributions serves as one of the keys to being pronounced—by the "Great Mentioner" (the opinion-making elite)—a viable candidate. Hubert Humphrey, no stranger to campaign financing, said the following concerning the need to beg for money during a campaign:

> Campaign financing is a curse. It's the most disgusting, demeaning, disenchanting, debilitating experience of a politician's life. It's stinky, it's lousy. I just can't tell you how much I hate it. I've had to break off in the middle of trying to make a decent, honorable campaign and go up to somebody's parlour or to a room and say, "Gentlemen, and ladies, I'm desperate. You've got to help me. . . ."
>
> And most likely one of them is in trouble and is somebody you shouldn't have had a contribution from."[107]

Finally, the hoops we make candidates jump through may not be a functional and they certainly aren't a very dignified way to select the leader of the free world. The selection process may appear to be a survival of the fittest contest, but it is really a personality and money-collecting contest, in which the skills needed to govern are rarely tested. Of course, the ultimate test of a selection process is the type of president who emerges from this system. In recent years the new president has tended to be inexperienced in, unprepared for, and incapable of governing at the top level.

✪ THE MARKET AS PRISON

Presidential politics operates within an economic framework of *corporate capitalism*. How does this reality shape and influence presidential behavior?

Two major functions of the modern capitalist state are the stimulation of material *accumulation* and the *legitimization* of the social order. The first function derives from the fact that the state is ultimately held responsible for meeting the material needs of the society; thus, at least in some minimal terms, economic deterioration is blamed on presidents. But in this regard the capitalist state is "weak," in that it does not own the means of production; they are privately held and will not be put in operation unless a return (profit) on investment is foreseen. Thus, the capitalist state must use the carrot more than the stick, by helping the owning class in the accumulation of profit in order to promote production. Conversely, the owning class is in a strong position with presidents, who face the likelihood of an "investment strike" if policy is seen to hurt profits. This gives business a privileged position and places the president in a position of some dependency on what is referred to as "business confidence." In order to govern effectively, presidents must please the business community, lest they face a decline in business confidence and a deterioration of the overall economy, thus leading to a decline in presidential popularity and power.

It is just this situation that Charles Lindblom—though not referring specifically to the presidency—discusses in his article "The Market as Prison."[108] Lindblom argues that political regimes with market systems have built-in defense systems that automatically trigger punishment whenever there is an attempt to tamper with or alter the basic structures of such systems. This built-in punishing mechanism makes market systems resilient and highly resistant to change because attempts at change bring quick and sure punishment. As Lindblom writes, "Many kinds of market reform automatically trigger punishments in the form of unemployment or a sluggish economy."[109] This punishment is not the result of any conspiracy on the part of business; it is simply a built-in by-product of market oriented systems. Lindblom writes:

> Business people do not have to debate whether or not to impose the penalty. They need do no more . . . than tend to their own business, which means that, without thought of effecting a punishment on us, they restrict investment and jobs simply in the course of being prudent managers of their enterprises.[110]

While Lindblom does not focus on the presidency in this context, he does discuss the notion that the economic system is highly resistant to change by political leaders. He describes the situation thus:

> What about government officials? It is critical to the efficiency of automatic punishment that it be visited on them. For it is they who immediately or proximately decide to persist in policy changes or to withdraw from such initiatives. The penalty visited on them by business disincentives caused by proposed policies is that declining business activity is a threat to the party and the officials in power. When a decline in prosperity and employment is brought about by decisions of corporate and other business executives, it is not they but government officials who consequently are retired from their offices.
>
> That result, then, is why the market might be characterized as a prison. For a broad category of political/economic affairs, it imprisons policy making, and imprisons our attempts to improve our institutions. It greatly cripples our attempts to improve the social world because it afflicts us with sluggish economic performance and unemployment simply because we begin to debate or undertake reform.[111]

Thus, with policy making being "imprisoned" in market-oriented systems, the leverage of presidents for reform is severely restricted by this self-regulating, self-punishing mechanism built into the system.

The other function, legitimization of the social order, derives from the need for the state to be seen as ruling in the interest of all, not in the interest of a dominant class. Welfare programs for the nonowning classes and entitlement programs for the middle class are examples of policies to satisfy this task. But when profits are squeezed, the revenues to support such programs become tight, and a crisis for the state can occur because it cannot reach an adequate balance between these contradictory goals.[112]

Edward S. Greenberg develops the notion of the privileged position of business in policy making in these words:

> Presidents must act in such a way that they maintain the confidence of business leaders and ensure an economic environment conducive to profitable investment. The president's popularity and thus much of his ability to effect a domestic program and foreign policy objectives is dependent on the state of the economy and the sense of well-being felt by the American people.
>
> Since business people cannot be forced to make productive, job-creating investments in the American economy, government must induce them to do so. They are induced, in the main, by public policies that encourage and ensure profitability, especially among the most powerful economic actors and enterprises in the system. Thus, while no president can afford to respond to every whim of important business leaders, all his actions are bounded by the need to maintain "business confidence."[113]

There is no active conspiracy on the part of business to "capture" the presidency. Rather, presidential success is intimately connected with business success. As presidential popularity rises and falls, in part due to economic conditions, presidents quickly learn that what is good for business is usually good for presidential popularity.[114] When corporate capitalism gains, the president usually gains. Conversely, a sluggish economy is blamed on an administration's activities or lack thereof. Thus, the fate of the president is closely connected to fluctuations in the economy. Presidents help themselves by helping business.[115]

In this way, presidents who do not have the confidence of business find themselves at a distinct political and economic disadvantage. As John Kennedy noted:

> I understand better every day why Roosevelt, who started out such a mild fellow, ended up so ferociously anti-business. It is hard as hell to be friendly with people who keep trying to cut your legs off. . . . There are about ten thousand people in this country involved in this—bankers, industrialists, lawyers, publishers, politicians—a small group, but doing everything they can to say we are going into a depression because business has no confidence in the administration. They are starting to call me the Democratic Hoover. Well, we're not going to take that.[116]

But Kennedy recognized the other side of the business confidence coin as well, as he attempted to act as economic cheerleader when he said,

This country cannot prosper unless business prospers. This country cannot meet its obligations and tax obligations and all the rest unless business is doing well. Business will not do well and we will not have full employment unless there is a chance to make a profit. So there is no long-run hostility between business and government. There cannot be. We cannot succeed unless they succeed.[117]

Similarly, presidents who wish to pursue a reform agenda find themselves in a bind: "Do I sacrifice economic reforms for economic performance and personal popularity, or, do I play it safe and hope for incremental changes?" Which president would want to stir the embers of the market's self-punishing mechanism? Which president could afford to stir the beast that will likely produce a sluggish economy and lower presidential popularity? Thus, presidential leverage in economic reform is severely limited by the invisible prison of the market.

Thomas Cronin, probably the most highly regarded of today's presidential scholars, begins to suggest a structural impediment in presidential choice vis-à-vis the business community when, in a lengthy reexamination of Richard Neustadt's *Presidential Power*, he chides Neustadt for failing "to take into account the degree to which presidents are almost invariably stabilizers or protectors of the status quo rather than agents of redistribution or progressive change." Cronin adds that "all our presidents have had to prove their political orthodoxy and their acceptability to a wide array of established powers, especially to corporate leaders. . . ."[118]

Political scientist Bruce Miroff notes that presidential scholars remain firmly committed to a "progressive" interpretation of the presidency. But as Miroff writes, "The Presidency, even (perhaps especially) in liberal hands, is best understood as the chief stabilizer—and not the leading force for change—in American politics."[119] No president has "sought to question, much less assault, corporate power and its extraordinary skewing of resources and rewards. The present structure of the American economy has been accepted by modern Presidents as a given of American life."[120]

In line with Charles Lindblom's concerns, Miroff writes:

Because of their acceptance of the prevailing social and economic order, even the more liberal of recent Presidents have had little novel or profound that they really wanted to achieve in domestic affairs. Their most controversial domestic proposals have envisioned only modest reforms. Basically, these Presidents have sought to patch up remaining holes in the New Deal, and to stabilize and rationalize the corporate economy. None have acknowledged more fundamental problems in American society; none have proposed anything that resembles a program of social and economic reconstruction. Contrary to the conventional view, it has not been an obstructionist Congress or an apathetic public that has kept Presidents since FDR from major domestic accomplishments as much as it has been the orthodoxy of their own domestic vision.[121]

Presidents are thus constrained by the needs of corporate capitalism. They are in part imprisoned, limited in what they can do, by the requirements of accumulation and legitimization.

✪ THE POLITICS OF DECLINE

If presidential politics operates within a restricting economic framework, presidents are bound by a dramatically changing international framework as well. With the end of the Cold War, the old road maps that guided leaders have been replaced by chaos and confusion. Presidents—who could once rely on ample resources, the deference of others in the making of policy, and a clear (if sometimes mistaken) policy road map—now face a more confusing world, armed with more limited resources and confronted by more challengers to their position of power and decision making.

A presidential problem unique to the modern period is the relative decline of America's international power. In the immediate aftermath of World War II, the United States emerged as *the* superpower of the world. It was the beginning of what was called "the American Century." The United States was seen as a leader, its resource base was unmatched in the world, and it assumed hegemonic control of the West.

The emergence of the United States as world leader did not go unchallenged. The Soviet Union emerged as a rival, be it a relatively weak one, to U.S. hegemony. This competition led to the Cold War, and in the United States, to the development of the National Security State. The combination of U.S. international power and the development of the national security state in the Cold War led to an era of expansive presidential power.[122]

But by the early 1970s, cracks began to show in U.S. hegemony: economic challenges from Japan and Europe and military challenges from the Soviet Union led to an erosion of U.S. power.[123] The United States no longer had its massive margin of superiority. The "rise of the rest," U.S. economic woes, a diffusion of international power, as well as a host of other troubles beset both superpowers. This led to the demise of the Soviet empire and the decline of U.S. power: an Age of Limits.[124]

One cannot discuss the rise and relative decline of U.S. power without mention of the presidency and presidential power. Inexorably linked to the rise of the American empire has been the rise of presidential power. The United States has become, for better or worse, a presidential nation, with economic and military power under the limited command of the president. This does not mean that the traditional checks and balances provided by the Congress have evaporated. But it has become clear that the burden if not always the resources of leadership has fallen on the shoulders of the president. When leadership occurs—and the system is often mired in gridlock—it is almost always the president who provides the momentum in the system. In the absence of presidential leadership, stagnation is almost guaranteed. This is especially true in foreign affairs. Thus, the formulating of policies to deal with the age of limits rests with the president.

If the United States is to successfully negotiate the choppy waters of an age of limits, presidential choice and presidential leadership will be the keys. Sound policies can arrest relative decline; unwise policies will accelerate decline. The age of limits is a two-edged sword, and one must ask: how will the age of limits affect the presidency, and how can the presidency affect U.S. power in this age? Richard Rose in *The Postmodern President: The White House Meets the World* suggests that the presidency is going through a profound change, so drastic that he sees the emergence of a "Postmodern Presidency."

Rose sees three distinct stages in the development of the presidency. In the first stage, the Traditional Presidency (1789–1932), the office was relatively weak and Congress dominated the political landscape. Local politics predominated, and the presidency was not the center of power. In the second stage, the Modern Presidency (1932–1976), the power of the presidency grew. National politics dominated as the depression and World War II thrust the United States and the presidency into the limelight. Foreign policy became more important and the presidency became the center of action.

But Rose sees a third stage of development in the office, in which *"the resources of the White House are not sufficient to meet all of the President's international responsibilities"* (emphasis in the original). As Rose notes, for the postmodern president to succeed, he must win not only the support of the public and Congress but of other nations as well. No easy task in an era of relative decline.[125]

The essential "difference between the modern and the postmodern Presidency is that a postmodern President can no longer dominate the international system."[126] This is so essentially because *interdependence* reduces the ability of a hegemonic power to control or direct events. As Rose notes:

> The President is the leader of a very influential nation, but other nations are influential too. . . .
>
> While the White House is accustomed to influencing foreign nations, the postmodern President must accept something less appealing: Other nations can now influence what the White House achieves. Whereas the Constitution made Congress and the Supreme Court the chief checks on the traditional and the modern President, the chief constraints on the postmodern President are found in other nations.[127]

Rose sees the postmodern presidency first rising during the war in Vietnam, and by the mid-1970s the transition from modern to postmodern state is complete. To Rose, Jimmy Carter was the first truly postmodern president. How has the transition to postmodern status affected the presidency?

"A generation ago," writes Rose, "the President had a trump card in dealing with foreign nations: to act as if they were not there." Presidents no longer have that luxury. "Whatever a postmodern President would like to believe, he soon recognizes that there are now few problems of significance to him that can be resolved by unilateral American action."[128]

The postmodern president must generate support from and the cooperation of three very different audiences: the American public, the American Congress, *and* the international audience. The president does this from a position of some strength but not dominance. He is more vulnerable and less powerful. Rose and other presidential scholars see a transformation in presidential power as the president faces more demanding problems with fewer tools and resources. As Rose notes, "A postmodern President must start from the assumption: To *govern is to cooperate.*"[129]

✪ CONCLUSION

There are, one can see, a variety of good reasons why presidents rarely perform up to public expectation. Some of the blame rests with individual presidents who lack sufficient political skills. Part of the blame rests with the structural design of the American constitutional system that separates and fragments power. And as this chapter points out, there are a variety of other permanent and temporal roadblocks that inhibit presidential leadership.

The American presidency, public misperceptions to the contrary, is in many ways a very limited office with limited powers. The president faces heavy responsibilities and high public expectations with limited political resources. For presidents, the presidency is not a very user-friendly institution. It should not surprise us that disappointment in presidential performance is commonplace.

The result is (usually) presidential paralysis, political gridlock, and public cynicism. Historically, this problem is not new. In other eras, other presidents have faced gridlock and political fragmentation. But in recent years, this paralysis has taken on a new tone of urgency. With the relative decline of U.S. power, the demise of the Soviet empire, the dramatic changes taking place in the post-1989 world, and the evaporation of political consensus at home, the need for creative political leadership is high.

But some presidents *do* lead, *do* move the machinery of government, *do* succeed. Why? How are we to explain presidential success? What magic do those few great leaders work on the lethargic American system? We now turn our attention to the strategies presidents can employ to heighten their chances of political success.

✪ FOR DISCUSSION

1. Were the Founders right? In creating the American system of government and in inventing the presidency, were they correct about (a) human nature; (b) the need to control power; (c) the utility of a separation of powers system; (d) the rule of law and limited government; and (e) the amount of power given to the president in the Constitution?

2. The Founders wanted to prevent tyranny and limit governmental power. Today, we need more efficiency; we need to run the government like a business. Discuss.

3. Is the United States really in (relative) decline? If so, how will this affect presidential power?

4. Is America's political culture *really* anti-leadership and antiauthority? Isn't most of the nation conformist and obedient to their rulers? Is American culture too individualistic and consumer oriented?

5. Does capitalism imprison the president, or, does America's great wealth liberate a president, free him to do great things?

6. What tests of character and competence should our presidential selection system impose on candidates? Are "private/personal" issues (such as a candidate's sex life) relevant to presidential selection?

✪ DEBATE QUESTIONS

I.   Resolved: That the presidency is too big a job for one person to handle.
II. Resolved: That the public expects and demands too much of its presidents.

Chapter 3

PRESIDENTIAL POWER MAXIMIZING STRATEGIES

And now for something completely different.

—Monty Python

If "successful presidents" seem to be an endangered species, it is for good reason: most presidents do not succeed, are not able to overcome the lethargy built into the system, cannot bring sufficient skill to bear on the limited opportunities they face. But some presidents *do* succeed; some of the time they do get their way; some do win. Why? What makes a successful president successful? What do they do that other presidents don't or can't?

To be successful, a president must be a jack of all trades *and* a master of all! Since power floats in the United States,[130] since it is so elusive, a power vacuum is the natural order. But power abhors a vacuum, and someone or some thing fills it. Usually, the vacuum is filled by those who wish to protect the status quo: as the protectors of what is, they have most of the advantages over the advocates of change. In the United States, there is a great deal of *negative power*, multiple veto points, but there are few opportunities to promote change.

Many rivals attempt to fill the power void, but no one is better situated to do so than the president. By what means can a president fill that power vacuum? By the creative force of presidential leadership. Presidential leadership, as used here, refers to more than mere office holding. Leadership is a complex phenomenon revolving around *influence*—the ability to move others in desired directions. Successful leaders are those who can take full advantage of their *opportunities, resources,* and *skills*. Institutional structures, the immediate situation, the season of power, the political culture, the regime type, and the dynamics of followership define the *opportunities* for the exercise of leadership. The *resources* at a leader's disposal include constitutional and statutory powers, intermediaries, the media, the level of popularity, the nature of the congressional majority, and the policy arena. It is easy, however, to mistake resources for power. A successful leader converts resources to power, but it is not automatic. To convert resources to power requires skill.

The leader's *skills*—his style, political acumen, experience, political strate-gy, management skills, vision, ability to mobilize political support, character traits, and personal attributes—provide a behavioral repertoire, a set of com-petencies. Opportunities, resources, and skills interact to determine the potential for success or failure in attempts to lead and influence.[131]

A president who can play to the optimum the cards of opportunity, resources, and skill has a chance of succeeding. Such a leader can resemble Superman or Leviathan rather than Gulliver tied down by thousands of lesser figures. But unusual is the president who maximizes power. More often, the president resembles the helpless giant.

The presidency, as popularly understood, can't work. Our expectations are too high and the president's powers are too thin: so many roadblocks, so few useful road maps; so many veto points, so few avenues to power. As Thomas E. Cronin has written, "Their [presidents'] responsibilities exceed their meager powers."[132] The surprise shouldn't be that most presidents can't lead effective-ly; the surprise is that some do lead. We cling to the romantic myth of FDR and ask, Why can't they all do what he did?

But few presidents are FDR, and few face the opportunities for leadership that FDR enjoyed. Power is dispersed; it "exists only as a potential. Leadership is the means by which the president can exploit that potential. This is no easy task."[133]

The president has vast responsibilities, with overwhelmingly high public expectations but limited power resources. But as an institution, the presiden-cy has proven to be somewhat elastic; it stretches to accommodate skilled leaders in situations of high opportunity, but it also contracts to hem in less-skilled leaders. Noting the variable nature of the power potential in the presi-dency, Robert Dahl has written: "The Presidency is like a family dwelling that each new generation alters and enlarges. Confronted by some new need, a President adds on a new room, a new wing; what began as a modest dwelling has become a mansion; every President may not use every room, but the rooms are available in case of need."[134]

The variable nature of presidential power has left presidency scholars somewhat schizophrenic regarding the proper scope and limits of presidential power. As presidents performed credibly (1930s to early 1960s), scholars called for an enlarged institution. But as presidents faltered (1960s to 1980s), they called for restrictions on presidential power. This variability is reactive; it is based on the subjective judgments derived from the political performance of presidents. But such evaluations miss the key point: the *normal* state of the presidency is one of constrained power. To be successful, presidents must overcome nature, or at least, the nature of power built into the system. Thus, for our purposes, it is better to look at the requirements for leadership gener-ically—at the preconditions necessary for the exercise of political leadership—than merely to react to the current temporary occupant of the White House. By doing this we can see not only how well a particular president performed but also which threads, or common factors, run through the presidency.

Generically the presidency is a relatively weak institution. The president is especially vulnerable (to outside veto points) and dependent (on others to go along with him). His independent powers are quite limited. It is an office of enormous responsibility, extravagant expectations, but limited power. How do presidents make up for this power shortage? How do they lead?

It should be noted that while the Founders sought a governing structure that was slow, deliberative, and multifaceted, they also wanted a government that could (with some difficulty) *act*. Yes, the Founders wanted a government of energy, but a specific type of energy—energy that resulted from *consensus* and *cooperation*. What model or type of leadership is required to move such a system?: a model based on *consensus*, not fait accompli; *influence*, not command; *agreement*, not independence; *cooperation*, not unilateralism. Such a model of power requires presidents to think strategically, to play a complex game.[135]

If the model of leadership built into the presidency is one of cooperation and consensus, what paths are open for presidents to lead? Under what conditions can a skilled president take a relatively limited office and exert leadership? What are the fuels that ignite presidential power? What are the preconditions of successful presidential leadership?

✪ PRESIDENTIAL LEADERSHIP

The President is at liberty, both in law and in conscience, to be as big a man as he can. . . . His capacity will set the limit. . . .

—Woodrow Wilson

I claim not to have controlled events, but confess plainly that these events have controlled me.

—Abraham Lincoln

In the social sciences, the words *leadership* and *power* are often used interchangeably. This is a mistake. Leadership suggests *influence*; power is *command*. Leaders inspire and persuade; power-wielders order compliance. Leaders induce followership; power-holders compel or force acceptance. Officeholders have (to some degree at least) power merely by virtue of occupying an office. Leaders, on the other hand, *earn* followership. The officeholder uses the powers granted to his official position. The leader tries to reshape the political environment; "he seeks to change the constellation of political forces about him in a direction closer to his own conception of the political good."[136]

On occasion, a president can act on his own authority, "independent" of other political actors. President Bush's 1989 decision to overthrow the government of Manuel Noriega in Panama is an example of this form of power. But such unilateral acts as this are the exception, not the rule. In most cases, presidents share power. Therefore, leadership, the informal "powers" so eloquently elaborated upon by Richard Neustadt, becomes so important to presidents who wish to promote political change.

All presidents have some power, some ability to command. But such power is short-term and limited. It ceases to exist when the president leaves office. Its effects can often be undone by a new president.

A president's formal power—for so long the focal point of presidential studies[137]—includes constitutional authority, statutes, delegated powers, and those areas in which others follow a president's command. But with the publication of Richard Neustadt's influential *Presidential Power* in 1960,[138] the more informal power to persuade took center stage in presidential studies. Rather than take an either-or approach to the debate over formal versus informal powers, we should see these two potential sources of strength as complementary, as presidential options in the pursuit of their goals. While presidents derive some of their powers from constitutional sources, they derive others from political and personal sources. Effective presidents use *all* the resources available to them. They assess the situation and determine where are their best chances for success, and they are flexible enough to make the adjustments necessary to optimize their power. In short, effective presidents are able to adjust their dance to fit whatever music is played.

True leadership occurs when presidents are able to exploit the multifaceted nature of opportunities both to command *and* to influence. In his classic study, *Leadership*, James M. Burns suggests that leadership takes place when

> persons with certain motives and purposes mobilize, in competition or conflict with others, institutional, political, psychological, and other resources so as to arouse, engage, and satisfy the motives of followers. . . . Leadership is exercised in a condition of conflict or competition in which leaders contend in appealing to the motive bases of potential followers.[139]

For better or worse, only presidential leadership can regularly overcome the lethargy built into the American system and give focus and direction to government. Congress can, on rare occasion, take the lead on a policy, as was the case when the Congress overcame presidential opposition from Ronald Reagan and imposed economic sanctions on the white minority government of South Africa. But such cases are infrequent. Congress simply is not institutionally well designed to provide consistent national leadership over extended periods of time. In the second half of the twentieth century, the citizens have most often looked to the White House for leadership and direction. If the president doesn't lead, gridlock usually results. In this sense, John F. Kennedy's view that "The presidential office is the vortex into which all the elements of national decision are irresistibly drawn"[140] rings true. Presidential leadership remains the key for moving the machinery of government. But, given all that is arrayed against him, how can presidents lead, and not merely preside?

✪ THE BUILDING BLOCKS OF PRESIDENTIAL LEADERSHIP

Out of the multitude of factors affecting any president's ability to lead, only two are really within his personal purview. These two elements—the president's vision and skill—provide the foundation upon which the president's potential for leadership rests. Given the limits established for the institution of the presidency, these matters of vision and skill—all the possible power that generates from the president himself—are also the starting points of our attempt to answer this question: How, then, must the president—for better or worse—act to direct *and* lead the way against the plethora of demands pressing downward upon his center of power?

Vision

Beyond question, the most important "power" a president can have is the ability to present to the public a clear and compelling *vision*. A well-articulated, meaningful, positive vision that builds upon the building blocks of the past, addresses needs and hopes of the present, and portrays an image of a possible future opens more doors to presidential leadership than all the skills and other resources combined. A moving vision can transform a political system, can recreate the regime of power, can chart a course for change. Vision energizes and empowers, inspires and moves people and organizations. A president with a compelling vision can be a powerful president.

Few presidents use what Theodore Roosevelt referred to as "the bully pulpit" to develop a public philosophy for governing. Rather than attempting to educate and lead the public, most presidents seem content to serve as managers of public business. But if presidents wish to craft change, and not merely preside, they must use the bully pulpit to promote a moral and political vision in support of change.

A visionary leader, akin to what James M. Burns calls a transforming leader,[141] gives direction to an organization, gives purpose to action. Visionary leadership charts a course for action. Such leaders are both instruments for change and catalysts of change.[142]

When asked how he worked, Albert Einstein replied, "I grope." Groping may be acceptable for a genius of Einstein's caliber, but presidents must do more than grope; they must lead. Of course, the reality is that most presidents merely grope and are thus mere officeholders. But groping is not enough; holding office is not enough. And one of the essential differences between a leader and a mere officeholder is that leaders have a vision, communicate that vision, and animate the public and Congress through expressions of that vision. As leadership expert Burt Nanus of the University of Southern California writes, "There is no more powerful engine driving an organization toward excellence and long-range success than an attractive, worthwhile, achievable vision of the future, widely shared."[143]

Effective leaders, in government, business, and public organizations, share a common trait: they are visionaries. Nanus writes:

> There is no mystery about this. Effective leaders have agendas; they are totally results oriented. They adopt challenging new visions of what is both possible and desirable, communicate their visions, and persuade others to become so committed to these new directions that they are eager to lend their resources and energies to make them happen. In this way, effective leaders build lasting institutions that change the world.[144]

Visions do not spring full blown from the belly of the leader. Developing a vision involves the ability to consider "existing realities as transformed possibilities."[145] Visions are enabling and empowering. They are derived from the core values of a community, flow from the past, are about the future. Visions inspire, give meaning and direction to a community, are road maps. Visions are about achieving excellence.

A vision is an idea, a dream of the future, a dream that is realistic enough to appear attainable, different enough to inspire, attractive enough to gain consent and commitment. It is about hope: this is what tomorrow can be, this is what it looks like, this is how we can get there, this is the cost, and this is our ultimate reward. A vision grabs your attention, stirs your imagination, appeals to what is best in us.

"Leaders," write Bennis and Nanus,

> articulate and define what has previously remained implicit or unsaid; then they invent images, metaphors, and models that provide a focus for new attention. By so doing they consolidate or challenge prevailing wisdom. In short, an essential factor in leadership is the capacity to influence and organize meaning for members of the organization. . . . Communication creates meaning for people. Or should. It's the only way any group, small or large, can become aligned behind the overarching goals of an organization.[146]

Visionary leaders are remembered and continue to have an impact long after they leave office. For example, it has been over thirty years since John Kennedy was killed, and over twenty-five since the death of Martin Luther King, Jr., and yet the memories of their leadership—the power of their ideas and the impact of their words—remain powerful forces in the contemporary political arena.

On a smaller and decidedly opposite political scale, Ronald Reagan was able to mobilize and inspire his followers because he was skilled at presenting his vision to the public. In contrast, George Bush, who admitted he wasn't big on "that vision thing," was a singularly uninspiring officeholder, and weeks after his leaving office, he had all but faded from political memory. Why is Reagan's presence still felt while Bush has become invisible? Vision.

No other actor on the political scene is better positioned to present a vision to the public than a president. Already the focus of much media and public attention, presidents can become "highlighters" of important issues to be addressed as a part of the president's vision. While presenting a somewhat more limited role, political scientist Lester Salamon has written that presidents need to develop

> a more strategic approach to the office, one that conceives of the president not as the ultimate decision maker but as the preeminent "national highlighter," whose most important task is not to settle all issues, but to identify a handful of issues of truly national importance and focus on them the attention, visibility, and support that only a president can provide. Such a role is far more consistent with the unique advantages of the office . . . and far more compatible with the capabilities of the institution and the demands of the job.[147]

Skill

The general public seems to assume that skill is all that is necessary for a president to be successful. If only we could get another FDR—so the belief goes—we could make things work. Wrong.

Skill is important but skill is not enough. Even the most skilled individuals face formidable roadblocks. Skill helps determine the extent to which a president takes advantage of or is buried by circumstances, but circumstances, or the political environment, set the parameters of what is possible regarding leadership. President Reagan used to refer to the "window of opportunity," his way of talking about how open or closed were the circumstances for exercising presidential leadership. For example, a skilled president who faces a closed window—such as the opposition party's controlling the Congress during a period of economic troubles in which the president's popularity is low—will be very limited in what he can accomplish. In contrast, a president of limited skill who has an open window of opportunity will have much greater political leverage, even though his skill base is smaller. It is thus entirely possible for a president with limited skill to be more successful than a president with great skill. If one is dealt a weak hand, there is only so much that skill can do. But if one is dealt four aces, *fortuna*—not skill—determines outcome.

Again, this is not to say that skill is unimportant. It does make a difference. But in the constellation of factors that contribute to success or failure, skill is but one, and it is probably not the most important element.

At election time one often hears political cynics whine, "It doesn't matter who gets elected; they all end up doing the same thing anyway." Social science lends *some* support to this cynical view. After all, we social scientists widely believe that the *institution, role, expectations*, and other conditions play a significant part in determining behavior. But while the cynic has a point, it should not be taken too far. Individuals are constrained, but to an extent, individuals *do* matter.[148]

Another way of looking at the skill versus opportunity dilemma is to focus on what is referred to as a president's "political capital." Is a president's capital like a bank account, in which a one-time deposit is made at the beginning of his term, and must he then invest carefully and draw on that account prudently, lest he run out of resources? Or, can a president add to his bank account from time to time, renewing his resources?

George Bush seemed to think that his capital was a fixed sum, and in spending it, he dissipated his capital. Bill Clinton, on the other hand, does not view his political capital as a fixed asset. He regularly spends, then tries to replenish his assets. As President Clinton has noted,

> even a President without a majority mandate coming in, if the President has a disciplined, aggressive agenda that is clearly in the interest of the majority of the American people—I think you can create new political capital all the time, because you have access to the people through the communications network. If you have energy and sort of an inner determination that keeps you at the task, I think you

can re-create political capital continuously throughout the Presidency. I have always believed that.[149]

Princeton political scientist Fred Greenstein sees the presence of the following factors as making a situation especially bendable to individual variations: (1) ambiguity; (2) an absence of standardized "mental sets" or roles; (3) a lack of sanctions attached to an action; (4) a presence of high intensity of personal feelings or beliefs; and (5) an involvement of high-skill-based actions.[150]

There are, thus, certain situations where the individual, not the institution, dominates. Do leaders make a difference? Yes, sometimes. As Erwin C. Hargrove writes, "Surely the issue is not, Do individuals make a difference? but Under what conditions do they make a difference? The relative importance of leaders varies across institutions and across time and place. . . . The task of scholarship is to integrate the study of individuals with the social and institutional forces that move them and that they, in turn, may influence."[151]

When do individuals matter? When is skill an important variable in presidential success? While it may sound obvious, it is nonetheless important to note, as Hargrove does, that "effectiveness in achieving goals was enhanced if skill and task were congruent."[152] To that I would add a third element: opportunity level. Skill matched to task when the window of political opportunity is open usually leads to goal attainment. Hargrove himself recognizes the importance of opportunity when he writes, "The impact of individual leaders on events and institutions is greater or lesser depending upon the historical situation and the opportunities available to them."[153]

The stamp of individual presidents who made a difference in specific policy areas is unmistakable: Lyndon Johnson and the war on poverty, Richard Nixon and China, Jimmy Carter and human rights, Bill Clinton and gun control, and so on. These presidents had choices, moved in new directions, made a difference. Their options were limited, but they were able in these areas to overcome the natural lethargy of the system and succeed in selected policy arenas. The fact that presidential behavior in most areas and on most issues appears more similar than dissimilar should not obscure the fact that—on some issues at some times—some presidents *can* make a difference.

The attempt to determine what role skill has played in these events remains a slippery task. Could any president have opened doors to China? Probably not. Could any president emphasize human rights in his foreign policy? Probably. So where are we? When does skill matter? How can we recognize or measure political skill? Lamentably, it is probably too elusive a concept to wrestle to the ground. Suffice it to say that high levels of skill, task congruence, and opportunity usually lead to presidential success, and low levels of the aforementioned usually lead to failure.[154]

Begging the question: If skill is of *some* (unmeasurable) importance, it might be useful to ask, what skills are most useful to a president? *Political experience* is often touted as a requirement for effective leadership, and while this sounds like good common sense, the correlation between experience and achievement is not strong.[155] After all, some of our most experienced leaders were our biggest failures (Nixon). But overall one could argue that more experience is better than less experience, although it is by no means a guarantee of successful performance. While Washington, D.C., "amateurs" (Carter, Reagan, and Clinton) have made serious blunders in part due to their lack of experience, experienced political hands (George Bush had the best résumé in Washington) have often done poorly despite their backgrounds. This suggests that while experience *can be* very helpful, there are other factors that to a great degree determine the success or failure of a president.

Both the Reagan and Clinton presidencies serve as excellent examples of D.C. amateurs behaving amateurishly in the White House. Reagan in Beirut, and Clinton in Somalia, placed American military personnel in harm's way, without sufficient support or protection and against the recommendations of many experienced advisers. In both cases, Americans were ambushed, leading to the death of over 220 marines in Beirut, and a dozen in Somalia, before changes in policy led to increased safety precautions. In both cases, leaders with no foreign policy experience made tragic blunders that could have been and should have been avoided. More experienced hands probably would have known better.

Political skills are always in short supply, and the president who has a high level of political acumen can sometimes gain the upper hand. By political skill we mean a good sense of *timing* (to know when an issue is "ripe"—when to move, when to hold back); *task competence*; a *power sense*; *situational skills* (crisis versus routine-decision skills); *policy skills* (to develop sound workable programs); and *political savvy* (to love playing politics, as FDR did, not hate politics as Nixon did). Of FDR's love for politics, James M. Burns has written,

> If other leaders bent under the burdens of power, Roosevelt shouldered his with zest and gaiety. He loved being President; he almost always gave the impression of being on top of his job. Cheerfully, exuberantly, he swung through the varied presidential tasks. . . . The variegated facets of the presidential job called for a multitude of different roles, and Roosevelt moved from part to part with ease and confidence.[156]

To be successful, presidents also need *people skills*. Presidents must know how to persuade, bargain, cajole, and coopt. They must be masters of self-presentation. They must be able to motivate and inspire, to gain trust and influence. Charisma helps. In short, occupants of the White House must master the art of "presidential schmoozing."

Personality skills also loom large in the arsenal of presidential requirements.[157] All presidents have a drive for power. For some, it is held within healthy bounds; for others, Nixon for example, it destroys a president. To be effective, presidents should be self-confident, secure, flexible, and open. Presidents who are consumed by self-doubt, insecurity, rigidity, and a closed personality (Barber's "negative" characters) are often dangerous and apt to abuse power.

Related to this, presidents also need *self-knowledge*. We all have our weaknesses, but we do not all let our weaknesses consume us. By recognizing his or her strengths *and* weaknesses, a good leader can attempt to deal constructively with weakness, come to grips with failings, offset the negative. For example, a president who is inexperienced in foreign policy may need to compensate by surrounding himself with very experienced foreign policy insiders.

Managerial skills, sometimes referred to as *process skills*, are also extremely important if a president is to succeed.[158] This set of skills is dealt with separately and is merely mentioned here.

Finally, a president must have *personal style skills*. By this I mean he must be disciplined, have great stamina, high intelligence, sound judgment, and maturity. Good presidents are creative, empathetic, and expressive. They have a sense of optimism that gives people reason to hope. And they have a sense of humor. Ronald Reagan's self-effacing sense of humor served him well as president; it disarmed opponents and won over much of the public.

✪ POLITICAL TIMING

The "when" of politics matters greatly: when major legislation is introduced, when the public is ready to accept change, when the Congress can be pressured to act, when the president leads and when he follows, when he pushes and when he pauses. A sense of political timing, part of the overall "power sense" all great leaders have, helps a president know when to move, when to retreat; when to push, when to compromise. Primarily, there are two elements of political time most germane to the leadership dilemma of a president: the *transition* and the *honeymoon* period.

The Transition

Getting a good start is a key element of political success, and during the transition—the eleven-week period between the November election and the January inauguration—some of the most important work of an administration is done.[159] In this preparation stage before taking office, the president-elect lays the groundwork for much that is to follow, and he sets the tone that shapes the way others see the new administration. During the transition, the president-elect must, in essence, make all of the following key decisions: who will be the top advisers, who will fill important cabinet positions, and how will the staff be structured; what decision-making (management) style will he employ; will he pursue a partisan strategy or else try to woo the opposition; how will he mobilize the public; and what issues will the administration push during the first year. Much like the journalist's key questions, these five *w*'s (who, what, when, where, why) and an *h* (how) of politics set the stage not only for how the administration will operate but also for the way the public, Congress, and media will view and respond to the new administration. The Clinton transition—slow, awkward, drifting—was seen as an opening by the Republicans and the press to jump on the new president earlier than is customary. Thus, Senator Bob Dole (R., Kansas) led a highly orchestrated series of early attacks on the new president, designed to undermine his leadership. Likewise the press, sensing disarray (and wishing to show bipartisanship after Republican attacks on the media), jumped all over themselves in an effort to find negative things to say about Clinton.[160]

The transition is thus important because, as James P. Pfiffner points out, "power is not automatically transferred, but must be seized. Only the *authority* of the presidency is transferred on January 20; the *power* of the presidency—in terms of effective control of the policy agenda—must be consciously developed."[161] Thus Pfiffner suggests that in order to seize power, presidents must adopt a strategic approach to the transition, one that leaves little to chance and that deals self-consciously with seizing and using power.

Of Honeymoons and (Un) Happy Marriages

Gerald Ford, upon taking office in the midst of the Watergate scandal, said he wanted a happy marriage, not just a honeymoon. He got neither. The marriage between a president and Congress is a mixed marriage that rarely turns out to be a happy one over the long haul. Therefore, presidents need to get all they can as early as they can before the marriage slips into bickering and sniping. To do this, a strategic president does all he can to take advantage of the honeymoon period. The honeymoon is a brief period of time, lasting anywhere from roughly three to ten months (or, for Clinton, three to ten minutes), immediately following a presidential election, when the public, press, Congress, and others begin to give the president the benefit of the doubt, go soft on him, refrain somewhat from criticism, and are most likely to vote for measures proposed by the president. The president "claims" an electoral mandate; the opposition, uncertain of how strong the new president will be, usually goes easy on him; and everyone is waiting to see if indeed the new guy will seize power. In short, the vultures are not yet circling the president's carcass. Thus, the president is often at the peak of his power in his honeymoon period.

As Lyndon Johnson said, "You've got to give it all you can, that first year. Doesn't matter what kind of a majority you come in with. You've got just one year when they treat you right."[162] And the best way to get as much as you can, early, is to have a short, disciplined agenda, focus exclusively on that agenda, and push, push, push.

Presidents are more likely to propose new programs in their first year in office than at any other time. Their success rate with Congress in the first year is usually the highest of their term. The irony here, as Paul Light points out, is that presidents are at their strongest when they are least knowledgeable.[163]

To take advantage of this potential to exercise power during the honeymoon, a president must strategically approach his transition and early weeks of the new administration with a clear game plan, a focused mode of presentation, a short, disciplined agenda, and an unceasing sense of political pressure on the system.

It is considered wise to select a few big issues in the early going and to focus all attention on attaining those goals. The difference here, between

Ronald Reagan on the one hand, and Jimmy Carter and Bill Clinton on the other, is striking. When Reagan took office, his administration very self-consciously chose to focus on a select few big-ticket items: a tax cut, for example. All other issues, including important foreign policy matters, were put on the back burner (which infuriated Alexander Haig, the new and short-lived secretary of state).[164] This allowed the Reagan administration to devote all its energies to hitting a select few legislative home runs, and it also conveyed an image that this president could succeed, could get his way, could win. He appeared to be, and for a time was, powerful.

By contrast, both Carter and Clinton had large, unyielding legislative agendas. What did they want? Everything, it seemed, and nothing. They could not decide what was most and what was least important. President Clinton, when he should have been focusing attention on his economic stimulus package in early 1993, instead got sidetracked by the issue of gays in the military. This issue may have been important, but in the big scheme, it ranked well behind the economic stimulus package. Where Carter and Clinton seemed sprawling and unfocused, Reagan maintained a short, disciplined issue focus.

Overall, Clinton had a very shaky start. In the early going he suffered defeat on his economic stimulus package, fumbled the Haitian refugee issue, backed away from his middle-class tax pledge, blundered on several early cabinet appointees, and was indecisive on Bosnia-Herzegovina and Somalia. At the time when Clinton was supposed to be at his strongest, he kept shooting himself in the foot. And the Democrats in Congress, unaccustomed to having a compatriot in the White House, at the first smell of presidential blood seemed instinctively to form a circle for a firing squad. It was not a pretty sight. It is amazing that, in spite of his shaky start, President Clinton has been able, time and again, to recover and even to snare a few wins. While he missed opportunities in the honeymoon, he recovered and was able to win significant victories on a budget resolution and the Brady (gun control) Bill. When he later stumbled on the Whitewater affair, again he came back, winning a tough fight in the House to bar certain assault weapons. Next, when he faced persistent questions relating to his character and charges of sexual harassment by Paula Corbin Jones, he focused his attention on health care reform.

In the honeymoon period, a president must "hit the ground running"[165] by concentrating on a few key policy issues, work hard to cooperate with (even coopt) Congress, focus public attention on his agenda, promote himself and his program, seize center stage, control the agenda, and set the terms of debate. That's all. . . . But that is the time when the president's window of political opportunity is often open fairly wide, and a skilled president can drive his legislative program through the system. In the United States, and in other systems, the early part of a new leader's term often finds the most significant political changes occurring.[166]

In some ways, the honeymoon comes at the best of times: following an election, with a promise and hope for change, an air of optimism. In other ways, however, it comes at the worst of times. Under normal circumstances the president is at his peak of power when he is least able to cope with the demands of office: he is new, inexperienced, learning the ropes, most prone to error or misjudgment. Paul Light recognizes this when he writes of how a president's power is high during the early stages of his term but, due to what he calls "the cycle of decreasing influence," will erode over time. Though the president's "cycle of increasing effectiveness" makes him more skilled or adept later, yet over time his power declines.[167] When a president is most capable he is least powerful, and when he is least capable, he is most powerful. The dilemma was recognized by President Reagan's first Office of Management and Budget Director David Stockman, who feared a "GOP Economic Dunkirk" if quick action wasn't taken.

> Things could go very badly during the first year, resulting in incalculable erosion of GOP momentum, unity and public confidence. If bold policies are not swiftly, deftly and courageously implemented in the first six months, Washington will quickly become engulfed in political disorder commensurate with the surrounding economic disarray. A golden opportunity for permanent conservative policy revision and political realignment could be thoroughly dissipated before the Reagan administration is even up to speed.[168]

The problem, of course, is that Reagan did pass dramatic tax reduction legislation and increase defense spending dramatically, thus driving the federal budget to the brink of economic insolvency. Presidents are thus most prone to make mistakes when the system is most likely to follow their lead.

But presidents are in some ways prisoners of time and must make the best of what they are handed. They are usually handed (apart from a crisis) the most power when they are least adept. Thus, to hit the ground running becomes an essential ingredient for presidential success, just as that same success in those early days can often lead to major blunders.

Scholars point to the Reagan honeymoon as an example of how to make the most out of early opportunities. Reagan combined an attractive personality with a compelling television presence and a vision that he articulated masterfully, and he focused on only a few key issues. But he was a poor planner and weak manager. During his transition, his key advisors put together—with little involvement from the president-elect—a narrow, focused agenda and initiated a public relations and legislative blitzkrieg that ended in the president's gaining almost all of his early legislative agenda. This in turn added to the aura of power surrounding Reagan and made it easier for him to win subsequent contests because the Congress "feared" Reagan.[169]

A key factor in adding to a president's power during the honeymoon is the nature of the previous presidential election: can the president claim an "electoral mandate"? If so, he will have an easier time getting his program passed by Congress. Therefore, the nature of the presidential campaign is very important. A mandate is based on three features: the size of a president's electoral victory; the type of election (issue oriented or personal); and the number of the president's party elected to Congress (the president's coattails and the aggregate numbers). Ronald Reagan serves again as an excellent example of both the benefits of a mandate and the absence of such.

In 1980, Reagan ran a campaign in which he discussed issues. He laid out a clear vision, discussed his proposed changes, and paved the way for his agenda. After the election he claimed a mandate and was able to convince the public and some wavering Democrats in Congress that his way was the way the nation had to move. During his early months in office, Reagan focused attention on a few select issues, pushed hard, and won some big victories. He was successful because the conditions were right and the strategy appropriate.

But during his 1984 reelection bid, Reagan ran a purely personal, issueless campaign. He ran on personality, not policies. Thus, in spite of his winning a huge electoral landslide, it was widely seen as a victory for the man—not the ideas—and when, during his second term, Reagan went to the public and Congress with his proposals, he was soundly rebuked.

Finally, where timing is concerned, Machiavelli reminds us that *fortuna* also guides our fates. Luck, good and bad, plays a role in presidential leadership. For example, Jimmy Carter had the bad luck of being president at a time when the oil-producing nations (OPEC) clamped a stranglehold on the West by sending the price of oil through the roof. This caused the economies of the developed nations to plunge into a tailspin of low productivity and high inflation.

By contrast, Ronald Reagan had the good fortune to become president at a time when OPEC was breaking up and oil prices shot downward. This picked up the economies of the developed nations and cooled inflationary pressures. Thus, through no effort of their own, Carter's popularity suffered (Carter reminded us of the old blues song, "If it wasn't for bad luck, I wouldn't have no luck at all") and Reagan's was aided by events beyond their control.

✪ CONTROLLING THE AGENDA

The president's top job, as stated earlier, is to articulate and promote a *vision* for the nation's future. Presidents must identify the national purpose, then move the machinery of government in support of that vision.

Goal-oriented presidents control the political agenda; they take charge, are masters and not victims of their fate. To have a chance to control the agenda, a president must (a) develop and articulate a compelling vision; (b) present a series of policy proposals designed to achieve that vision; (c) sell it to the public and Congress; and (d) place emphasis on the presentation of self and programs. If accomplished with skill and timing, this program *may* allow the president to control the political agenda and thereby to make the rest of the political system dance to his music.

While opportunity often shapes the parameters of permissible presidential actions, presidents do have some control over their fates. But in setting the agenda, the president must always remember that other officials and interest groups have their own priorities, and that they compete with the president for control of the agenda. While the president may be the center of attention, he is only one of many actors vying for attention.

Think of the presidents who had an impact, who dominated the political landscape. They may not have been the "best" presidents (e.g., Reagan), but they were the ones who mattered, who won, who got their way. Of course, one thinks of FDR and Reagan. Both dominated the issue agenda, refashioned the debate, forced the rest of the system to respond to their initiatives.

Reagan presents an interesting case in agenda control because he was probably the most ideological president of this century. And Reagan's extreme conservatism helped him develop a clear vision, a policy agenda, and an action program. There is a good and a bad side to being an ideologue. It can be good in that a strong ideology can simplify complex problems; on the bad side, some problems (most problems) do not lend themselves to simple solutions. On the good side, ideology gets the administration marching in the same direction; on the bad side, they may be marching like lemmings, over a cliff. Ideology highlights certain variables in problem solving; at the same time, it hides or obscures other equally important variables. Finally, ideology gives passion to purpose; it can also degenerate into crusading extremism.

By contrast with the ideologues, Bill Clinton, a political moderate, must attempt to re-create himself on every issue. His being more moderate and pragmatic may help him avoid the mistakes of either extreme, but it creates problems of its own. It is difficult to develop a vision and generate a committed following around being moderate. While it may be easier for political moderates to *get* elected, it may be harder for them to set visions and govern.

Because power in the American system is floating, a policy entrepreneur can, on certain issues, capture control of the policy agenda. If this can be done, a president may be able to force an otherwise reluctant Congress to at least meet him partway on his policy goals. And no one is better positioned to attract attention than the president. If he is to lead and not merely preside, the president must control the agenda. If the agenda escapes him—as it seemed to do early in the Clinton presidency—he appears weak and distracted, which may force him into a reactive, not a proactive, mode.

Of course, the nature of the issues at hand matters greatly. For example, in 1981 Ronald Reagan was selling a massive tax *cut* to the public. Does it take a political genius to sell a 33 percent tax cut? Promising candy is easy and popular. But poor Bill Clinton, attempting to be more responsible, tried to tell the public what it needed to hear (tax increase), not what it wanted to hear (tax decrease). Whose job is tougher?—that of Reagan, who promises the people candy, or of Clinton, who offers sour-tasting medicine?

The late Speaker of the House of Representatives Thomas "Tip" O'Neill reminded us that the "most important power is to set the agenda."[170] And early in his term, Bill Clinton lost control of the agenda. He failed to focus, did not narrow his agenda down to manageable size, seemed distracted. Learning from his early mistakes, by September of 1993 Clinton regrouped and put a full-court press on the health care reform issue. He gave a major speech, had photo opportunities related to health care for the next several days, sent his lieutenants out to make the rounds on the issue, and shaped the debate. Health care was debated on *his* terms. He controlled the agenda, for a time at least.

✪ COALITION *AND* CONSENSUS BUILDING

The model on which the American system of government was founded is based on consensus and coalition building. Consensus means agreement about *ends*; coalitions are the *means* by which the ends are achieved. Since power in our system is fragmented and dispersed by design, *something* (usually a crisis) or *someone* (usually the president) has to pull the disparate parts of the system together.

In other words, power can only be legitimately exercised when the different parts of the system are acting together. Since power floats in the American system, it has to be harnessed and channeled. For this to happen, a consensus on what to do has to be developed, and a coalition of forces has to be formed.[171]

A consensus can be formed *if* the president has a clear, focused agenda and can forcefully and compellingly articulate a vision, and *if* the public is ready to embrace that vision. If a president can develop a consensus around his vision, he can then muster the power to form the coalitions necessary to bring that vision to fruition.

Simply placing a legislative package at the doorstep of Congress is not enough, as President Carter so painfully learned: presidents must work to build support within and outside Congress. As Thomas E. Cronin notes,

> The office does not guarantee political leadership; it merely offers incumbents an invitation to lead politically. It is in this sense that those best suited to the job are those who can creatively shape their political environment and savor the rough-and-tumble give-and-take of political life.[172]

To govern in the United States is to build coalitions, to form alliances and power networks. There are relatively few areas in which a president can act unilaterally and not face at least a few challengers to his authority. Custom and the design of the U.S. system necessitate coalition building by political leaders.

Of course, this is easier said than done. The centrifugal force of American politics pulls the system apart, encourages independent entrepreneurship. Power is not fused as it is in parliamentary democracies; instead, the president and the Congress are elected in campaigns that are relatively independent of one another, and political parties do not develop a great deal of cohesion among the branches. Political scientists Benjamin Ginsberg and Martin Shefter agree that since elections fail to provide clear governing coalitions, the president and Congress end up resorting to "politics by other means" in order to influence policy.[173] Institutional combat, not power sharing, characterizes this relationship because both branches attempt to usurp power and govern autonomously. Of course, this usually leads to conflict and/or gridlock.

This dilemma highlights the essential difference between what it takes to get elected and what it takes to govern. Getting elected requires the development of an "electoral coalition." Governing requires the development of a "governing coalition." These may be very different, even contradictory things.

This difference between electoral and governing coalitions was noted by presidency scholar James MacGregor Burns, who has written that "there's an increasing disparity between the tests for winning office and what's required in governing. The kinds of quick, dexterous ploys, mainly public relations ploys, that are called for in public campaigning are a very far cry from the very solid coalition building that is needed to make this system of ours work."[174]

To get elected, Bill Clinton made appeals to a wide variety of traditionally Democratic interest groups, hoping to pull a sufficient number of these groups together to ensure his election. It was a successful electoral strategy. But was it good for governing? As soon as the election was over, all these groups approached Clinton, *demanding* that he keep his promises and deliver the goods. Clinton tried to deliver on his promises and, for example, broadened federal support for abortion rights (which garnered some backlash); he also attempted to allow openly gay persons to serve in the military. These two issues generated a tremendous backlash as opposition from the military and fundamentalist religious groups all but paralyzed the new administration in the honeymoon period, and these early and highly publicized controversies did significant political damage to the new president precisely at the time he should have been at his power peak. In effect, Clinton's honeymoon was in part sacrificed at the altar of his electoral coalition.

To govern, presidents must go to Washington and play the politics of the beltway, that small area surrounding Washington, D.C., which is sometimes seen (usually by political losers) as an alien culture. Governing requires the *skills* of "presidential schmoozing": pressing the political flesh, deal making, cajoling, trading, bargaining, persuasion, negotiation. It involves being feared and loved, playing what James M. Burns calls the lion and the fox; it involves being a politician. And all good politicians are coalition builders. It is the difference, journalist Hedrick Smith notes, between "outside politics" and "inside politics."[175] Smith writes further:

> In the campaign game, the winning presidential candidate builds a personal organization, but the successful president must work effectively with other organizations. He must work with other factions in his party, his party's national structure, the leadership in Congress, sometimes the opposition. Indeed, several recent presidents failed because of their inability to deal effectively with rival power centers: Kennedy and Carter, unable to forge durable governing coalitions in Congress; Nixon, Johnson and Reagan, overreaching for power, usually in disregard of Congress because they did not want to deal with organized opposition or modify their positions to gain wider support. The contrast between campaigning and governing is, ultimately, the difference between stagecraft and statecraft.[176]

The political party *can* serve as an aid in coalition building. In 1981, Ronald Reagan relied on a unified Republican party to help push his program through Congress. President Clinton has spent a good deal of time lobbying congressional Democrats on behalf of his agenda, but the Democrats remain a fractured and combative lot (they wouldn't be Democrats if it were otherwise), and Clinton has had a very difficult time keeping his majority together in Congress.[177]

Because Clinton has an ambitious agenda but only a thin congressional majority, and because the opposition party was, in the first six months of Clinton's term, amazingly unified *against* the president, Clinton was forced to rely on the Democrats alone for votes. This has emboldened some Democratic legislators, who feel they have leverage with the president and can trade favors for votes. (Clinton's strategy, however, paid off early; he won nearly 90 percent of the votes in Congress.)

✪ POPULARITY

Leading the public is believed to be one of the key sources of power for a president. But the ability to move the nation and generate public support takes time and effort; it is not automatically conferred at the inauguration, nor is it always translated into political clout. Presidents spend a great deal of time and effort trying to build popular support both for themselves and their programs. Usually their efforts come to very little.[178]

A president with popular support (and other skills to complement popularity) can exert a great deal of pressure on Congress and is more likely to get his program passed.[179] As a result, presidents are keenly aware of fluctuations in popularity, and they routinely engage in efforts aimed at dramatizing themselves in the hope of increasing their popularity.

Popularity as a Source of Power

It is widely believed that popularity is a very convertible source of power, that presidents can convert popularity into congressional votes, better treatment by the media, and less criticism by political opponents. While hard evidence to support these claims is scarce, one must remember that, in politics, *perception* counts more than *reality*. If a president can convince the Congress that he is popular and therefore powerful, and that to defy him is politically dangerous, the battle is half won. In his first two years in office, this is precisely what Ronald Reagan was able to do. Democrats in Congress were afraid that Reagan's popularity might really have been as wide and as deep as Reagan claimed, and they therefore were more likely to vote for his legislative proposals and less likely to take him on frontally. The perception of power thus gave Reagan more power.

But we must not make too much of Reagan's, or any other president's, ability to move public opinion. After all, on one of the issues nearest and dearest to Reagan's heart—aid for the rebels in Nicaragua (the Contras)—Reagan failed, despite herculean efforts, to sway the public or Congress to support his goals. In the end, Reagan was forced to act unilaterally and illegally to attain his goal, but he was never able, despite his much deserved sobriquet "the great communicator," to convince the public that they should accept his proposals.

Can presidents convert popularity into power? Political scientist George Edwards is skeptical. After a statistical study of the relationship of popularity to power, Edwards concluded that while popularity may help, there is no certainty that presidents who are popular will get their legislative programs through Congress.[180]

But in *Presidential Power*, Richard Neustadt puts a great deal of emphasis on public support as a source of potential power, seeing the absence of support as a great weakening agent:

> The weaker his apparent popular support, the more his cause in Congress may depend on negatives at his disposal, like the veto, or "impounding." He may not be left helpless, but his options are reduced, his opportunities diminished, his freedom for maneuver checked in the degree that Washington conceives him to be unimpressive to the public.[181]

Public support may empower presidents but is not an easy thing to attain. Abraham Lincoln knew well the potential power that rested in the hands of the public when he said, "Public sentiment is everything. With public sentiment nothing can fail, without it nothing can succeed."[182] And that is the challenge for presidents, to gain public support *and* convert it into political power. But as noted, public support is not always easy to attain nor is it always fungible. As Edwards and Wayne note, "The president is rarely in a position to command others to comply with his wishes. Instead he must rely on persuasion. A principal source of influence for the president is public approval of his performance and his policies."[183]

But how can presidents *lead* public opinion? Franklin Roosevelt asserted that "all our great Presidents were *leaders* of thought at times when certain historic ideas in the life of the nation had to be clarified," and his cousin Theodore Roosevelt observed, "People used to say of me that I . . . divined what the people were going to think. I did not 'divine.' . . . I simply made up my mind what they ought to think, and then did my best to get them to think it."[184] But how?

The more active and policy-oriented presidents are not content to let popularity settle at its natural waterline; they actively pursue popular support and thereby hope to add to their political capital. Presidents invest a great deal of time and energy in self-dramatization, information control, image management, media events, generating "pretty pictures" for television, giving carefully crafted speeches, relying on symbolism and ceremony, to the point that the "public relations presidency" has in many ways eclipsed the policy presidency in time and attention.

Of course, there is only so much a president can do. Even Ronald Reagan, the "great communicator," had his limits. While he had the ability to put the best possible light on a given situation, he could not reshape reality at will. As Jody Powell, President Carter's press secretary, noted,

> [With] Communications and the management of them, the impact is marginal. The substance of what you do and what happens to you over the long haul is more important, particularly on the big things like the economy. . . . Poor communications comes up after a problem is already there, if an economic program doesn't work, if it is ill-conceived, or if circumstances change. . . . The ability to turn a sow's ear into silk purses is limited. You can make it into a silkier sow's ear, that's all.[185]

The Public and the President

The president serves a variety of functions for the American public, and political scientist Fred Greenstein summarizes the psychological connection between the president and the people, noting that to the people, the president serves (1) as a symbol of national unity, stability, and the American way of life; (2) as an outlet for affect, for feeling good about America; (3) as a cognitive aid, simplifying complexity into a single symbol; and (4) as a means of vicarious participation in the political world.[186]

Because the president serves both as head of government (the nation's chief politician) and head of state (the symbolic representation of the nation), he is the chief divider of the nation as well as its chief unifier. Ronald Reagan was a masterful head of state, as evidenced in the aftermath of the Challenger disaster, when Reagan took on the role of high priest and national healer for a nation devastated by tragedy. This role, played so well by Reagan, added to his prestige and enabled him at once to reinforce his role as Reagan, the nation's top politician, and to rise above politics and become symbol for the whole nation.

Thus invested in the office of the presidency is high respect, but also high expectations (added to by presidential campaign promises). And yet, as noted in Chapter 2, the president's powers are not commensurate with his responsibilities or the public's expectations. This often leads presidents to frustration and also to declines in their popularity. In addition, if the public continues to demand that the government deliver on contradictory expectations (e.g., lower taxes *and* more government services), presidents are put in no-win situations. Given this dilemma, what's a president to do?

Theodore Lowi argues that presidents resolve this dilemma by resorting to rule by political manipulation. Impression management replaces policy achievement. Appearances are everything.[187] It is the president as the Wizard of Oz. The masters of the art of image manipulation were the handlers of Ronald Reagan. True, they had an excellent product to manage, but they masterfully played the media game, offering "pretty pictures" and staged events all designed to put the right spin on the situation. Brace and Hinckley maintain that this excessive reliance on appearances has led to the development of a "public-relations presidency . . . concerned primarily with maintaining and increasing public support."[188] In *The Personal President*, Lowi describes this development as "a plebiscitary republic with a personal presidency."

The President, the Public, and Democratic Theory

What is the proper function of the president as leader in our democratic system? Should he follow the public's wishes? Should he attempt to educate the public? Or should he attempt to *act*, to move the government in the direction he feels is best? Should the president find out what the people want and merely attempt to give it to them? Or should he speak truth (however unpleasant) to power?

The role of leader in a democratic society unveils a web of paradoxes and contradictions that can never be wholly resolved. And while the Founders feared a president who might fan the embers of popular passions,[189] it is clear that the "democratization"[190] of the presidency has led to the president's becoming the embodiment of the nation's government, making the president serve as a modern "interpreter in chief."[191]

Bruce Miroff writes eloquently of the "tension between leadership and democracy," arguing that for leadership to be democratic, the leader must have

> a respect for followers, rooted in a recognition of what Herman Melville called the 'democratic dignity' of every individual. . . . Democratic leaders want for followers what they want for themselves; their goals are egalitarian rather than exclusionary. Committed to the democratic belief in self-government, they understand that leadership must aim at engagement with followers rather than mastery. Yet engagement is a far cry from pandering; to nurture the democratic possibilities of citizenship, democratic leaders must be willing to question, challenge, even defy common conventions. In the face of the conventional antithesis between power and education, democratic leadership raises the possibility that dialogue between leader and followers can be mutually empowering.[192]

In essence, democratic leadership encompasses a moral vision with egalitarian goals. Democratic leaders question, challenge, and empower citizens. They engage in a dialogue with the people. They are educators.[193]

During his presidency, Jimmy Carter often attempted to educate the people on the limits of America's power, thereby treating the American public with the respect due an educated citizenry in a democracy. But Carter was unable to convince the public that it had to settle for less, make sacrifices, and accept limits. Or perhaps the public refused to listen, refused to believe, and blamed the messenger. This opened the door for Ronald Reagan, who mocked limits, scoffed at sacrifice. He promised the public easy, quick solutions to complex problems. He flattered the public and told them to buy, buy, spend, spend. They did. And at the end of the eight years of the Reagan presidency, the United States went from being the world's largest creditor nation to the world's largest debtor nation. Carter spoke of a tough reality; Reagan offered the public candy. Carter gave the public stagflation; Reagan offered a new approach. Carter lost; Reagan won. In the absence of war, calling for sacrifice seems to be a no-win proposition.[194]

The Vagaries of Presidential Popularity

If popularity is a potential power resource,[195] and if presidents spend a great deal of time and effort attempting to boost their popularity, one can fairly ask, how malleable is opinion to efforts at presidential manipulation?

Table 3.1 PRESIDENTIAL PUBLIC APPROVAL RATINGS, 1953–1994

PRESIDENT	TENURE	AVERAGE	HIGH	LOW	FIRST YEAR AVERAGE	FINAL YEAR AVERAGE
Clinton (year 1)	1993–94	49	59	38	49	NA
Bush	1989–92	61	91	32	65	40
Reagan	1981–88	52	68	35	58	57
Carter	1977–80	47	75	21	68	46
Ford	1974–76	47	71	37	75	48
Nixon	1969–74	49	68	24	63	24
Johnson	1963–68	56	80	35	78	40
Kennedy	1961–63	71	83	57	76	62
Eisenhower	1953–60	65	79	49	74	62
1953–63		68	83	49	75	62
1964–84		53.7	72	30	65	43

Source: Compiled from Gallup Polls, 1954–1994.

Between 1953 and 1965 (excluding only 1958), the average yearly presidential Gallup poll approval rating hovered at 60 percent or better. But starting in 1966, roughly the time when the most recent era of "failed presidents" begins, the level of popular support declines dramatically. Presidents who attained a 50 percent support level were unusual (see Table 3.1). In the age of failed leaders, the average yearly popularity of presidents has dropped roughly 10 percent. As public expectations for the heroic model of the presidency soared, a gap between what was expected and what was delivered helped create what might be called a "delivery gap." Greater expectations led to greater disappointments—no matter what presidents do, it isn't enough (e.g., Clinton's September 1994 agreement on Haiti met with as much criticism as praise). No wonder these presidents have a hard time leading.[196]

While public approval is the result of many factors, and while presidents can get a short-term boost in popularity during what are called "rally events" (e.g., international threats), it is also clear that over the long haul, popularity is the product of public judgments both over the way things are going generally and how the president is doing his job.[197]

Popularity or, more broadly, "prestige"—to use Neustadt's term—is shaped by a complex web of factors, but overall, the most important is the public's perception of the state of the economy.[198] The public will praise or blame the sitting president for the state of the economy, regardless of what a president does or does not do. Thus, when the economy is booming, presidential popularity rises; when the economy is in a bust, the president's popularity drops. Students of presidential popularity would do well to remember the advice posted on the wall of the Clinton campaign headquarters during the 1992 election: "It's the economy, stupid!" Candidate Clinton persistently focused attention on the sour state of the economy, knowing that George Bush (whether he deserved it or not) would be blamed for the slow economy.

If popularity equals (to an extent) power, and if efforts to manipulate levels of popular support are limited, presidents are caught between a rock and a hard place (the Bermuda Triangle of presidential politics). They must constantly be concerned (obsessed) with their popularity, and yet their ability to generate support is often out of their control. Gone are the days when Harry S Truman could publicly show his disdain for approval ratings with comments like

> I wonder how far Moses would have gone if he'd taken a poll in Egypt? What would Jesus Christ have preached if he'd taken a poll in Israel? . . . It isn't polls or public opinion of the moment that counts. It is right and wrong and leadership . . . that makes epochs in the history of the world.[199]

Polls and popularity ratings "have altered the time frame of democratic government, from quadrennial election to monthly review."[200] They force the president to dance to a different and much faster tune. With one eye always focused on popularity, presidents may be less likely to make the tough choices, the hard decisions.[201] Flattering the public has a greater short-term benefit than speaking a harsh truth.

The relationship between the president and the public he is to simultaneously serve and lead is a complex one. In order to govern, a president must have a fairly high level of popular support. But the avenues open to a president for attaining that support are limited. Public demands and expectations are high and often contradictory. The public wants presidents to deliver good news, not hard reality. (It is no accident that candidates with a message of hope and optimism are more successful than candidates of gloom and doom.) In order to lead, presidents must juggle twenty different balls at once. It is no wonder that so few are up to the job.

✪ THE MEDIA

Politically, the president is the nation's center of attention. But rarely can a president reach out and touch "real people." The media serve as the president's conduit for reaching the public. Through the media, especially television, the public sees the president, hears about his ideas, gets interpretations of how well or poorly he is doing his job. In this way, the media are, as Edwards and Wayne note, "the principal intermediary between the president and the public, and relations with the press are an important aspect of the president's efforts to lead public opinion."[202] Another way of putting it is that "Presidents cannot,"

Reprinted by permission: Vint Lawrence, *The New Republic*, June 21, 1993.

Harold M. Barger has written, "succeed without the media, but they have difficulty surviving because of the media."[203]

Because the president is the nation's center of political attention, public expectations are fueled and the impression is created that the president is more powerful than he is. The media's fascination with presidents, their families, their pets—one cannot walk down Pennsylvania Avenue in D.C. and not see kiosk after kiosk peddling "Socks, the President's Cat" T-shirts—has led to increased attention lavished upon the president, who serves as the nation's "celebrity in chief." The gravitational pull of the presidency gives the president a ready-made bully pulpit, but it also has a down side. In an era of hypercritical investigative reporting, everything and anything a president does is fodder for tabloid journalists. With TV talk shows such as Larry King and radio call-in shows with slash-and-burn DJs, we have an abundance of information but a shortage of knowledge. The micro coverage of the president trivializes the office, the man, and politics itself. Washington, D.C., has become Hollywood-on-the-Potomac, and the president becomes one more pop cultural icon. We have sunk to so low a level of media coverage of the presidency that two examples may reveal the absurdity of the president's dilemma.

On December 28, 1993, on the CBS Evening News, anchor Connie Chung reported that President Clinton had deducted from his taxes a charitable donation of three pairs of underwear. She then questioned whether the president deducted fair market value for the underwear, suggesting that he may have overvalued the deduction of underwear! The second example comes from the *Los Angeles Times* of April 8, 1994, in which the shocking story was reported of how President Clinton, while out jogging, slipped and fell in the mud and "soiled his long-sleeved white T-shirt, turquoise shorts and left leg." Is it news that when a president falls in the mud he soils his pants? Do we really need to know this? Do we even *want* to know this?

Presidents are too politically attractive to ignore. John Orman's study of periodical literature shows that Franklin D. Roosevelt averaged 109.5 stories per year of his presidency, John Kennedy averaged about 200, and Jimmy Carter averaged 407 per year. Ronald Reagan averaged over 500 stories per year.[204] By contrast, network news coverage of Congress has declined by roughly 50 percent between 1975 and 1985.[205]

This trend has both positive and negative consequences. But one thing is clear: it places the president at the center of media attention and elevates the president in the minds of the public. As Hedrick Smith writes:

> As a nation, we focus obsessively on the president, out of proportion with other power centers. This happens largely because the president is one person whom it is easy for television to portray and whom the public feels it can come to know. Other power centers are harder to depict: The Supreme Court is an aloof and anonymous body; Congress is a confusing gaggle of 535 people; the bureaucracy is vast and faceless. It is almost as if the president, most politicians, and the press, especially television, have fallen into an unconscious conspiracy to create a cartoon caricature of the real system of power. There is a strong urge for simplicity in the American psyche, a compulsion to focus on the single dramatic figure at the summit, to reduce the intricacy of a hundred power-plays to the simple equation of whether the president is up or down, winning or losing on any given day or week.[206]

Since the media serve as the president's conduit to the public, and because so much is riding on good press coverage, no president can afford to ignore, or even leave to chance, his relations with the media. Presidents must devise and implement strategies for attaining good press, and efforts at media manipulations are quite common.

This has led to the creation of what Thomas E. Cronin has called the "theatrical presidency,"[207] in which public relations specialists take precedence over policy people and style rules over substance. Reagan handler Michael Deaver (dubbed the "Vicar of Visuals") went so far as to admit that "image is sometimes as useful as substance."[208]

With the rise of the theatrical presidency has come an increase in efforts at presidential self-dramatization, at using public relations techniques and image management as a replacement for policy, at staging media events and framing the president in "pretty pictures" for the evening news. (During the 1988 presidential race it seemed impossible to turn on a television set and *not* see George Bush wrapped—literally and figuratively—in an American flag.)

Given that presidents are limited in what they can accomplish, and given that the public expects presidents to deliver the goods, sometimes, when faced with an inability to achieve policy results, presidents will resort to political grandstanding to give the impression that they are doing something. No administration used image management more often or better than the Reagan team. It is no overstatement to say that they were obsessed with image, and style was often used as a replacement for substance.[209]

In a perverse example of the tail wagging the dog, policy is often used for the public relations advantage it might deliver. And presidents can use selected pictures and images to erase political reality. At the time President Reagan proposed a cut in funds to assist the handicapped, the president went to a Special Olympics event and the pictures on the evening news showed a caring, concerned Ronald Reagan while the reality was that the president wanted to slash funding. And when polls revealed that the public disapproved of Reagan's civil rights policies, the president paid a very public (and media-filled) visit to a black family that had had a cross burned on its front lawn. (The cross burning occurred five years before Reagan's visit, but when one needs good visuals, what is a few years?) Reagan *appeared* to be concerned and caring. If his policies revealed an attempted reversal in civil rights enforcement, then his pictures had to supplant reality. It was the Wizard of Oz *before* Toto pulled back the curtain. If carefully managed, one picture truly can be worth a thousand words.

This obsession with image has forced presidents, in effect, to campaign 365 days a year. This permanent campaign has forced presidents to attempt to govern in a campaign mode. This means one must constantly paint pretty pictures for public consumption. As Hedrick Smith notes,

> In the image game, the essence is not words, but pictures. The Reagan imagemakers followed the rule framed by Bob Haldeman, the advertising man who was Nixon's chief of staff, the governing principle for politics in the television era: The visual wins over the verbal; the eye predominates over the ear; sight beats sound. As one Reagan official laughingly said to me, "What are you going to believe, the facts or your eyes?"[210]

Going Public

The image-management strategy of presidential power in the media age is called "going public." Samuel Kernell sees an unending political campaign in which presidents go public in an effort to increase political clout within the Washington community.[211]

In this, the United States has come a long way from what the creators of the presidency envisioned. The inventors of the presidency, as Jeffrey Tulis reminds us, feared a president who was too closely linked to the public because it might "manifest demagoguery, impede deliberation, and subvert the routines of republican government."[212] Such fears reflected the opposition to democracy shared by many of the Founders. Over time, such concerns gave way to the unstoppable logic of the electronic media and the need to use whatever levers a president could find to increase power.

Today, presidents go public because they have few other options. In a political landscape cluttered with the carcasses of failed presidents, an incumbent must use whatever resources are available, and governing by appearance, when governing by accomplishment fails, is something to which presidents often resort.

Managing the News

Upon entering office, presidents feel compelled to announce their intention of having an "open presidency." Such efforts are always short-lived. As James Davis notes, "News management follows on the heels of the so-called open presidency as the fall follows summer."[213] Presidents soon become concerned with the release of bad news, or leaked information, and begin to engage in news (or information) management.

Presidents can wield a carrot or a stick in dealing with the press, and some presidents revert to a "blame the messenger" strategy and attack the media. During the Nixon years, Vice President Spiro Agnew was used as the pointman in media attacks designed to (a) soften press coverage, (b) put the media on the defensive, and (c) plant seeds of doubt in the minds of the public so they would be less likely to believe press criticism of the president.[214]

While press harassment can have an effect, most presidents mix strategic approaches. In attempting to positively influence press coverage, presidents use a mix of strategies ranging from co-optation (Kennedy) to condemnation (Nixon).

It is important to link the media strategy to a president's political agenda. To do this, the president must coordinate the media strategy to the policy. In this, presidents would be advised to follow the Haldeman rule. As Richard Nixon's chief of staff, Bob Haldeman insisted that before something went on the president's agenda, or schedule, the staff member who proposed it had to tell (1) what the expected headline would be; (2) what the photo accompanying the headline would be; and (3) how the first paragraph of the story would read. The Reagan administration followed a variant of this model. Key aides met at 8:15 every morning to decide what the story of the day would be. They also developed long-term strategies for shaping the agenda.

By thinking strategically with a media focus, presidents can command media attention and shape coverage of the president's agenda. Presidents must choreograph every step, "wallpaper" stories with attractive visuals, and when things sour, send the spin doctors out to do damage control.

Walter Mondale may be partially correct when he says that the electronic media are largely to blame for turning the presidency into the nation's "fire hydrant,"[215] but the media are also a source of presidential power. There are times when the media are the lap dog for the president,[216] and at other times, the media check presidential power. If a president does not actively use the media, he may become their victim.

Whether the media are lap dog or power drain to a president depends on a variety of factors: the president's performance, his management of the news, events, the president's "charisma," and so on. But no president can casually approach the media. A clear strategy or game plan is needed if presidents are to dominate in this relationship.

Are the media biased? If so, are they biased in favor of the left or right of the political spectrum? During the twelve years of Republican presidents from 1980 to 1992, conservatives insisted that the press was out to get first Ronald Reagan and then George Bush. But was this charge accurate? The media do a strange mating dance when the president is the subject, and one may be inclined to level the charge of bias when one's preferred president is being criticized in the press. In point of fact, George Bush did get rough treatment from the media in 1992. If that is the point at which one measures bias, it might appear that indeed the press was out to get Bush. But if you choose a different point of time to measure bias, say, the first six months of the Clinton presidency, an entirely different picture emerges. Clinton was pummeled in the media during his first six months in office[217] (to a degree, deservedly). Less than two weeks into the Clinton presidency, ABC News's Sam Donaldson said, "This week we can talk about 'Is the [Clinton] presidency over?'"

Rather than look upon the media in a left-right fashion, it is probably more accurate to see the media as a herd. Generally, the media follow a herd mentality. When the president is up, they lay off (Reagan in 1984, Nixon in 1972); when the president is down, they gang up (Nixon in 1974, Bush in 1992, Clinton in early 1993).[218]

Overall, presidents dislike the press because it quotes them. But, to govern, presidents must work with and through the media, and presidents must think and act strategically where the media are concerned. Good press makes governing a bit easier; bad press makes governing all but impossible. The easiest way to get a good press is to do a good job. Failing that (and almost all presidents do), presidents often degenerate into efforts to control and manipulate the media.

✪ CONGRESS

Major Pierre L'Enfant, principal designer of the nation's capital, had more than space in mind when he located the president and Congress at opposite ends of the avenue. The Congress would be housed atop Jenkins Hill, giving it the high ground. The President would find his home about one mile away, at the end of a long street that would serve as a threadlike link connecting these two institutions. Not only did the Constitution separate the executive and legislative branches, but geography as well would keep these two branches apart.[219]

But for the U.S. system to work, both branches must find ways to bridge the gap, to join what is separated. The Founders saw the separation of powers not as a weakness (as we tend to see it today), but as a strength, as a way to ensure deliberation and thoughtfulness, as a way to prevent tyranny. But how does a president develop the syncopation of the branches necessary to make the system of separate institutions sharing power work? How can a president couple what the Founders decoupled?

Beyond question the relationship between the president and Congress is the most important one in the American system of government, and while the president spends a great deal of time and energy courting the media and appealing to the public, he does so in order to gain leverage with the Congress. For, in the long run, presidents must get Congress to formally or tacitly accept their proposals, lest they run the risk of deadlock, delay, or failure. After all, only Congress can allocate resources, and presidents who consistently attempt to go around the Congress cannot long succeed. The president may not like it, but he can't live without the Congress.

While there are a select few areas in which presidents may act semi-independently of the Congress, most of the president's goals require a partnership with Congress. This is no easy matter. As one longtime presidential adviser has noted, "I suspect that there may be nothing about the White House less generally understood than the ease with which a Congress can drive a President quite out of his mind and up the wall."[220]

In matters requiring legislative authorization, the Congress ultimately has the upper hand. Though the president may be seen as leader of the nation, agenda setter, vision builder, or legislator in chief, it is often the Congress that has the final say. And since there are multiple veto points in Congress, any of which may block a president's proposal, the forces wishing to prevent change almost always have the upper hand. The American system has many negative-veto points but few avenues for positive change.

In the expectations game, the president is supposed to dominate Congress. But public expectations notwithstanding, the president's legislative powers are constitutionally (Article 2, Section 3) quite thin. He has the veto power,[221] reports on the state of the Union, and extra-constitutionally may suggest legislation, lobby Congress, set the agenda, and build coalitions, but overall his *powers over* Congress are very limited.

In this sense, the Constitution sets up what Edward S. Corwin refers to as an "invitation to struggle" over political control of the Constitution (the power of the government). Another way to look at it is to see the Constitution as creating a situation in which "guerilla warfare" between the president and Congress is almost inevitable.[222] Since Congress has "all legislative powers" and the president has limited legislative powers, conflict is built into the system.

Originally (constitutionally) the Congress was established as the dominant branch of government, and the first few presidents were only minimally involved in the legislative process. But the Founders' vision soon gave way to political reality, and slowly presidents began to pull power into the White House, and generally the Congress was a willing participant in giving more and more power to the presidency. Today, as Robert Spitzer describes it, "What was designed as a congressionally centered system has evolved into a presidentially centered, or 'executive-hegemonic,' system."[223] Still, the Congress has a way of frustrating even the most skilled of presidents.[224]

While the image or expectation of the president is as "chief legislator" who "guides Congress in much of its lawmaking activity,"[225] the reality is quite different. The decentralized nature of the Congress, the multiple access and veto points within the congressional process, the loosely organized party system, the independent-entrepreneurial mode of the legislators, and the weakness of the legislative leadership all conspire against presidential direction and leadership.[226] As Edwards points out, this means that presidents impact Congress only "at the margins" and are more "facilitators" than leaders.[227]

Lest the system break down into hopeless gridlock, the president and Congress *must* find ways to work together. The theory upon which the U.S. government is based hinges on some cooperation between these two branches. As Justice Robert Jackson wrote in 1952, "While the Constitution diffuses power the better to secure liberty, it also contemplates that practice will integrate the dispersed powers into a workable government."[228]

Dealing with Congress

Under what conditions is a president most likely to establish his agenda and get congressional support? Put another way, when is the Congress most likely to follow a president's lead?

Several factors lead to presidential success when dealing with Congress. First, in a crisis, the president is accorded a great deal of deference, and the Congress usually backs up the president. Second, when a president has a clear electoral mandate (when the campaign was issue-oriented, the president wins by a wide margin, and the president's party has a sizable majority in Congress), the Congress sometimes will follow. Third, the president can exert pressure on members of Congress when he, the president, wins the election by a landslide *and* runs ahead of the member in his or her own district (this is usually referred to as "presidential coattails"). Part of President Clinton's problems with Congress can be traced to the fact that he ran behind most members in their districts, doesn't have a clear electoral mandate, and does not face a crisis.

Fourth, high levels of presidential popularity are often said to be a source of power over Congress. But how easily can presidents translate popularity into power? Many social scientists are suspicious, believing that popularity has only a marginal impact on presidential success within Congress.[229] But others argue that popularity does translate into power.[230] Richard Neustadt places a great deal of emphasis on presidential prestige as a source of power and influence, and his view is echoed by Stanford's Richard A. Brody, who writes that

> Presidential poll ratings are important because they are thought to be important. They are thought to be important because political leaders look for indications of when it is safe or dangerous to oppose their policy interests or career ambitions to those of the president and because indications of political support—which in other political contexts might be preferred—are too limited in scope to be relied upon in this context.[231]

Fifth, skill does make a difference, but how much of a difference? As is the case with popularity, scholars disagree about the importance of skill in legislative success, with some arguing that skill is of little importance,[232] while others see skill as very important.[233] Presidency scholar George Edwards warns that

> it is important to depersonalize somewhat the study of presidential leadership and examine it from a broader perspective. In this way there are fewer risks of attributing to various aspects of presidential leadership consequences of factors largely beyond the president's control. Similarly, one is less likely to attribute incorrectly the failure of a president to achieve his goals to his failure to lead properly. Things are rarely so simple.[234]

High skill levels can give a president greater leverage to win in the congressional process. Skills such as knowledge of the congressional process and needs; good timing, bargaining, deal making, persuasion, and coalition-building skill; moving the public, setting the agenda, self-dramatization, arm twisting, trading, consultation and co-optation, and even threats can all be used to advance the president's goals.

Lyndon Johnson, arguably the most skilled of the modern presidents vis-à-vis Congress—who also came into office on the heels of the martyred President Kennedy, won election by a huge landslide, and had a huge partisan majority and a shattered opposition in Congress—explained that there was only one way to deal with Congress:

> and that is continuously, incessantly, and without interruption. If it's really going to work, the relationship between the president and Congress has got to be almost incestuous. He's got to know them even better than they know themselves. And then, on the basis of this knowledge, he's got to build a system that stretches from the cradle to the grave, from the moment a bill is introduced to the moment it is officially enrolled as the law of the land.[235]

President Johnson perfected what came to be known as "the Johnson Treatment." Journalists Evans and Novak describe it as follows:

> Its tone could be supplication, accusation, cajolery, exuberance, scorn, tears, complaint, the hint of threat. It was all of these together. It ran the gamut of human emotions. Its velocity was breathtaking, and it was all in one direction. Interjections from the target were rare. Johnson anticipated them before they could be spoken. He moved in close, his face a scant millimeter from his target, his eyes widening and narrowing, his eyebrows rising and falling. From his pockets poured slips, memos, statistics. Mimicry, humor, and the genius of analogy made The Treatment an almost hypnotic experience and rendered the target stunned and helpless.[236]

Lyndon Johnson could be a presidential pit bull, but he was afforded that luxury only partly due to personal skills. He had, as mentioned earlier, other significant advantages that made his power more robust and his threats more credible (compare the resources Johnson had to the more meager power resources of a Bush or Clinton). One of the most important of these power resources is party support.

Partisan support in Congress is the sixth major factor shaping presidential success in Congress. Lyndon Johnson had such a large majority in Congress that, even if several dozen Democrats abandoned the president, he could still get his majority in Congress. George Bush, on the other hand, faced a Congress

The "Johnson Treatment" in action. Here, LBJ applies pressure to Democratic Senator Theodore F. Green: George Tames/NYT Pictures.

in the control of the opposition, and he was thus stymied in Congress. Bill Clinton has a paper-thin majority, and any defections could undermine his legislative hopes. This forced Clinton to do a great deal of vote trading and deal making with congressional Democrats in order to get his 1993 deficit-reduction bill passed by Congress as not one Republican voted for the president's proposal. In fact, deal making is a very common form of presidential leverage in attempting to extract votes from a recalcitrant Congress. Reagan Budget Director David Stockman noted that "the last 10 or 20 percentage of the votes needed for a majority of both houses on the 1981 tax cut had to be bought, period. . . . The hogs were really feeding."[237]

Related to this is the seventh factor: the nature of the opposition in Congress. How many votes do they have? How ideologically driven are they? How willing are they to work with the president? In 1981, President Reagan faced a Senate controlled by his own party but a House controlled by the Democrats. Reagan was able—via skill, luck, and circumstance—to win over enough Democrats (referred to as the "Boll Weevils") to win several significant legislative battles. By contrast, while President Clinton has majorities in both houses, the Republican opposition has been so ornery (Senator Dole of Kansas, in the first six months of Clinton's term, seemed determined to bring the Clinton presidency down) and so unified (on Clinton's 1993 economic package, not one Republican senator supported the president) that Clinton had an amazingly difficult time getting a win.[238]

Because of the nature of partisan politics, the eighth factor that shapes presidential success or failure in Congress is the nature of consultation between the two branches. One of the lessons President Clinton learned is that a president *must* consult, not only with his own partisans but with the opposition as well. There are so many veto points in the legislative process that attempting to gain cooperation and agreement must be the first step. If a president sets up an effective legislative liaison office and he can co-opt the Congress, he can often gain support (see Figure 3.1)

Source: Congressional Quarterly Weekly Reports, December 19, 1992, p. 2896.

Figure 3.1 Presidential Success in Congress.

Finally, the type of agenda a president pursues has a significant impact. George Bush had a very "thin" legislative agenda, and he pursued it only half-heartedly. Bill Clinton has a very ambitious agenda, making it more difficult to get the Congress to go along. This is made even more difficult by the fact that Clinton is proposing significant changes at a time when the economy is growing at a limited rate under stringent monetary controls. An ambitious agenda is difficult to pass in good times, but in tough times, the tough choices appear to be impossible choices.

In recent years, presidents have spent less time "going Washington" and more time "going public." The inside bargaining skills necessary to cut deals have been replaced by or supported by efforts at self-dramatization. In the loose bargaining regime of the Congress, presidents feel their time is better spent appealing directly to the public for support (which may translate into clout in Congress). But ultimately presidents must cut deals in Congress.

Initially, President Clinton's style of dealing with Congress was to use the "soft sell." Rarely did he twist arms or pressure legislators for a vote. This was partly a function of Clinton's preferred personal style of operating, but it also reflected his tenuous political position. Whereas Lyndon Johnson liked to and had the power to bully legislators, Clinton neither liked to nor did he have the power to get away with playing the role of presidential pit bull.[239]

But as the first year of Clinton's presidency drew to a close, the president changed form and as the vote on the North American Free Trade Agreement (NAFTA) drew close, Clinton showed great dexterity in dealing with Congress. With some he cajoled, with others he traded, with still others he applied pressure.[240] President Clinton demonstrated that, unlike most presidents, he could learn from his mistakes, develop a flexible style of "going Washington," and win major come-from-behind legislative victories.

Riding high in the aftermath of the NAFTA victory, Clinton was able to push a major crime bill through Congress, got the House to pass the controversial Brady Bill (a modest gun-control proposal), and began his push for health care reform. Overall, Clinton had a very good (early blunders not withstanding) first year in Congress, winning legislative support for his proposals roughly 90 percent of the time. By this measure, President Clinton had one of the more successful first years in modern history.[241]

Can presidents lead Congress? Yes, but not often and not for long. A mix of skill, circumstances, luck, popularity, party support, timing, and resources need to converge if the syncopation of the branches is to occur.

✪ MANAGEMENT

Political leadership is more than "great men" (persons) charting new territory and inspiring the masses to change. Leadership, in fact, rarely if ever follows the "great man/person" theory. True leadership does involve the promotion of vision. But it involves much more than this. Good management is also necessary if the leader is to succeed.

This raises the question: which dominates, the president or the presidency, the individual or the institution?[242] And how bendable are institutions to the will of individual presidents?[243]

The presidency is not just one man; it is also an institution. With the growth of the positive role of the federal government in solving the nation's problems, and with the growth of presidential responsibilities to accomplish these problem-solving tasks, the Institutional Presidency was born. So vast is the modern executive structure that most people see the presidency as unmanageable. The administrative duties of the presidency have risen enormously since the days of FDR, to the point that today the president is the unmasterful master of an enormous amalgamation that includes the White House staff, the Cabinet, the Executive Office of the President (EOP), and the bureaucracy.

The modern presidency is a collection of people in an institutional framework. How a president organizes his administration goes a long way in indicating what his interests, goals, and priorities are. But there are a number of potential pitfalls in presidential administration. Problems of sheer size and unmanageability, complicated issues and problems, competing demands for scarce resources, clientele demands, congressional controls, interagency competition, and a host of other problems await the president as Chief Administrator.[244]

There is a difference between leadership and management. Management is a subset of good leadership. Generally, good leaders are (must be) good managers, but not all good managers are good leaders. Many institutions are well managed but poorly led. As Bennis and Nanus write, "Managers are people who do things right and leaders are people who do the right thing."[245] Doing the wrong thing well is no bargain. Success at accomplishing bad things is not the goal of government. Warren Bennis sees the difference between leadership and management in the following manner:

- The manager administers; the leader innovates.
- The manager is a copy; the leader is an original.
- The manager maintains; the leader develops.
- The manager focuses on systems and structure; the leader focuses on people.
- The manager relies on control; the leader inspires trust.
- The manager has a short-range view; the leader has a long-range perspective.
- The manager asks how and when; the leader asks what and why.
- The manager has his eye always on the bottom line; the leader has his eye on the horizon.
- The manager imitates; the leader originates.
- The manager accepts the status quo; the leader challenges it.
- The manager is the classic good soldier; the leader is his own person.
- The manager does things right; the leader does the right thing.[246]

It behooves presidents to pay close attention to management. If a president wishes to see his policies and directives implemented, he will have to rely upon government agencies to faithfully execute his wishes. And as we know, presidential orders *are not* self-executing. Perhaps it is of greater importance that one could trace almost all of the major scandals and presidential blunders to failures of management. In the aftermath of the Iran-Contra scandal, the following joke made the rounds of Washington, D.C.:

Q: **What is the difference between a Day Care Center and the National Security Council under President Reagan?**
A: **A Day Care Center has adult supervision.**

One of the first questions a president must decide when putting together his administration is, How strong a chief of staff will he have? James P. Pfiffner, the leading academic voice of presidential management, argues that there are "two firm lessons of White House organization that can be ignored by Presidents only at their own peril: No. 1, A chief of staff is essential in the modern White House; No. 2, A domineering chief of staff will almost certainly lead to trouble." (Note, for example, Sherman Adams under Eisenhower, H. R. Haldeman for Nixon, Donald Regan for Reagan, and John Sununu for Bush.) Pfiffner concludes that "the preferred role for a chief of staff is that of a facilitator, coordinator, and a neutral broker."[247]

Apart from his selection of a chief of staff, a president must also decide how to organize that staff. There are a variety of different models one could follow: FDR's competitive approach, which set staff members off against other staff members in a dynamic tension; JFK's collegial style, which sought a cooperative, bonding approach; Nixon's hierarchical model, with a closed, rigid pyramid of access and line of authority; and Reagan's delegating style, which transferred power and authority to underlings.[248] Presidents tend to select a staff system based on (a) previous experience (Eisenhower chose a hierarchical model because he was accustomed to operating in a military structure) and (b) personality needs and preferred operating style (Nixon wanted a hierarchical system to protect him and keep him out of staff discussions).

There is no ideal organizational model. Each style of staff organization has costs and benefits. The key for the president is to know himself—his strengths and weaknesses—and to model his staff in a way that takes advantage of his strengths but also prevents his weaknesses from leading to serious mistakes. (See Box 3.1 for list of management skills needed.)

Williams's list is an excellent starting point which catalogues the key skills necessary for effective White House staffing. But it is the president's job to insure that the administration is both well led and well managed. In this the president has a number of options from which to choose.

While there is no "correct" staffing model, there are several things presidents must be aware of (see Box 3.1) lest they risk managerial (which translates into political) failure: (1) presidents need to spend time on managing; (2) presidents need to spend political capital managing; (3) presidents need a mix of old experienced White House staffers *and* some new fresh thinkers from the outside; (4) presidents need a devil's advocate close to the center of power

---

Box 3.1 Staffing Knowledge and Skills in a White House Policy Unit

1. **Integration capacity**—the ability to synthesize across policies and between policy and politics.

2. **Strategic thinking**—the ability to develop broad (macro) objectives, to analyze these objectives and the underlying assumptions as to consistency with other stated objectives and as to feasibility of implementation, and to refine and integrate these objectives.

3. **Process management leadership**—the ability to manage for the president (or his inner-circle designee) policy formulation or problem resolution in the executive branch.

4. **Policy analysis and quantitative techniques**—a mastery of the various policy analysis approaches and techniques and statistical techniques used by peer analysts inside and outside the government.

5. **Substantive (policy area) knowledge**—an in-depth understanding of particular policy areas, including relevant scholarly work, program and policy information, and analyses.

6. **Political knowledge**—an in-depth understanding of the political process, including the politics of particular substantive areas as manifested in the EOP, Congress, and federal agencies.

7. **Organizational knowledge**—an in-depth understanding of the organizational structure and bureaucratic politics of the agencies responsible for particular substantive areas.

8. **Monitoring**—the capacity to engage in efforts to ascertain how well policies and programs in the analyst's policy area are being implemented or managed.

Source: Walter Williams, *Mismanaging America: The Rise of the Anti-Analytic Presidency* (Lawrence: University Press of Kansas, 1990), p. 134.

---

whose job it is to poke holes in the ideas and programs that are proposed (all presidents need someone who can tell them to their face that they are screwing up); and (5) presidents need to be somewhat flexible in style.

Politicizing the Bureaucracy

Over time, presidents have a tendency to get suspicious, even paranoid, about the bureaucracy. The fear that members of his administration would, in Nixon aide John Ehrlichman's words, "go native" and represent the interest of the agency—and not the president—permeated the Nixon White House, and it is a view shared by many presidents.

As the nation's chief executive officer, the president is supposed to sit at the top of the bureaucracy and control its actions. But his control is incomplete at best. A president operates under a four-year time restraint; the bureaucracy has no such time constraint. The old saying "Presidents come and go but bureaucrats stay and stay" speaks volumes to the different time frames under which the president and bureaucracy operate. The president is the temporary occupant of the White House; the bureaucracy is part of the permanent government.

What approach should the president take in the management of the bureaucracy? Should he seek "neutral competence"—a nonpoliticized collection of experts? Or should he seek to politicize the levers of the administration, that is, to develop "responsive competence"—so as to promote responsiveness to the partisan and policy objectives of the president? This latter approach is characterized by Richard Nathan as the "administrative presidency strategy."[249] In this case the president, frustrated by the roadblocks Congress places before him, concentrates on an administrative strategy for accomplishing political goals. Given that Congress is unusually unresponsive, this method allows the president to bypass Congress and achieve through management and regulatory techniques what he could not get in the legislative arena.[250]

The model for a politicized bureaucracy was the Reagan administration. Facing a Congress controlled by the opposition, and wanting to implement a clear ideological agenda, Reagan was not content to rely upon the legislature to accomplish his goals. He employed an administrative strategy characterized by the self-conscious recruitment of ideological loyalists (Reaganauts, or "Reagan-nuts" as their critics charged); a focused ideological agenda, using administrative rule-making instead of legislative authorization; and, where necessary, a disregard for the law (the Iran-Contra scandal). The results were mixed.

While Reagan was able to accomplish some of his goals via an administrative strategy, the down side included a very high level of corruption (Iran-Contra, the HUD scandal, the sleaze factor); some ideologically sound but incompetent appointments (James Watt at Interior); and the creation of a backlash when Reagan's political end-run strategy came to light.

Good management requires time and effort. There is no administrative quick fix. The temptation of presidents to overly politicize the bureaucracy may seem to hold great promise, but it is fraught with dangers. Rather than settle for neutral competence or seek to overly politicize the bureaucracy, a strategy of responsive (but not politicized) competence seems the wisest course.

✪ POLICY ARENAS: FOREIGN V. DOMESTIC

Most scholars believe that there are significant differences in the institutional balance of power when one compares the realms of domestic and foreign policy. It is widely believed that presidents have greater power in the foreign policy arena than they do in domestic and economic policy.

In the mid-1960s, political scientist Aaron Wildavsky argued that since the end of the Second World War, presidents have been more successful at attaining their policy goals from Congress in foreign policy than in the domestic arena. Thus, Wildavsky concluded, there may be one president, but there are "two presidencies": one, a fairly powerful foreign policy presidency; the other, a fairly constrained domestic presidency. Commenting on the power of the presidency in the international arena, Wildavsky asserted that "there has not been a single major issue on which Presidents, when they were serious and determined, have failed."[251]

Initially, Wildavsky's thesis became holy writ. But recently, challenges to his thesis have emerged.[252] Wildavsky's data, so convincing when they were drawn from the 1950s and 1960s, were not as convincing in the post–Vietnam War era. After Vietnam, the Congress became more assertive and intrusive, and presidential leadership became more problematic. Even Wildavsky, by the late 1980s, has backed away from his two presidencies thesis, writing that "'The Two Presidencies' is time and culture bound," and also admitting that in his initial formulation, the thesis was very narrowly defined, with congressional voting patterns as *the* measure of proof.[253]

Indeed, by its narrowest measure, the Two Presidencies thesis does appear less plausible in the post-Vietnam era. But merely looking at congressional voting patterns does a disservice to the broader, richer opportunities of which presidents take advantage to get their way in foreign policy. Congressional voting is but one—and not the most important—measure of power in foreign affairs. Presidents, by virtue of their ability to act and preempt Congress, often have power over it. Presidents can act, make policy, be proactive, leaving the Congress behind. Congressional voting only measures a president's success *in* Congress. But so much is done *without* the Congress that in foreign affairs, presidents maintain considerable leverage over the legislature.[254] Indeed, there *are* two presidencies, and the foreign policy presidency, while not in absolute control of foreign affairs, does have a great deal of latitude in determining policy.

Even in the post-Vietnam era of political contention, divided government, and ideological division, presidents *usually* get their way in foreign affairs. For example, during the Reagan years, even though the Congress expressly voted to prevent Reagan from aiding the rebels (Contras) in Nicaragua, Reagan violated the law and ended up doing what he wanted anyway. This was possible because presidents have a variety of ways of accomplishing their foreign policy goals, apart from congressional enabling legislation. Presidents can merely *act*. "I make foreign policy," Harry Truman said, and indeed presidents are widely seen (the Constitution notwithstanding) as being the primary directors of foreign policy for the nation.

While Wildavsky's "two presidencies" notion may be a bit oversimplified, it does capture a certain element of truth. In foreign affairs, presidents can assert their will, act, and by being proactive, force the Congress to be reactive. By setting policy, the president sets in motion events of his choosing. If Congress wishes to intercede, it does so in response to acts already taken. The *initiative* usually belongs to the president.

Constitutionally, the president may be on shaky ground, but in practical terms, it is very difficult to stop an assertive president in foreign affairs. While all presidents claim that their use of foreign policy power is grounded in the

Constitution, such claims of independent authority are generally flimsy. It is the Congress—even in foreign affairs—that has the broadest and clearest constitutional mandate, but its power has atrophied due to lack of use. Even the power to declare war, which is expressly granted to the Congress, has slipped through the hands of the legislature. The War Powers Act notwithstanding, it is the president who holds primacy in war and foreign affairs.

The presumption of presidential leadership in foreign affairs gives the president a wide range of opportunities to take the initiative and act. It is *less likely* that Congress will challenge the president's authority in foreign than in domestic affairs (though it may be difficult to convince the president of this), and while the Congress is more intrusive today than in the 1950s and 1960s, the fact remains that presidents still can set the agenda, act, and lead in foreign affairs with much greater likelihood of success than in domestic matters.

A great deal of foreign policy involves diplomatic activities that are generally under the purview of the executive, and in most areas, presidents simply presume authority to act. Likewise, much activity in foreign affairs does not require legislation,[255] and, to make matters worse (or better if one is president), during a crisis the president acts with almost unlimited authority and very few checks.[256]

Perhaps the greatest power a president has is the presumption that he speaks for and represents the nation to the world. This allows the president the opportunity to act, to make decisions, to announce policies, thereby preemptively eliminating many potential challengers. By fait accompli acts, the president may tie the hands of potential rivals on the congressional side. To defy the president on a matter of national security *may* appear unpatriotic, especially in moments of international tension. Thereby, the president can both silence (or muffle) potential critics and force the Congress to submit to his will. Teddy Roosevelt's sending the U.S. fleet halfway around the world in defiance of congressional budget restrictions, then saying, "I sent the fleet . . . will they leave them there?"; George Bush's sending U.S. troops to the Middle East following the 1991 Iraqi invasion of Kuwait, preparing for war, building public support, *then* challenging Congress to issue a vote of support; and Clinton's sending U.S. troops to Haiti in 1993 serve as examples of how presidents, by acting and forcing the hand of Congress, can get their way.[257]

Over time, presidents spend more and more time dealing with foreign affairs precisely because they get frustrated after being rebuffed in domestic and economic policy but can feel a greater sense of power and accomplishment in foreign policy. Since a president needs to be seen as accomplishing great things in order to maintain his reputation as "the leader," he almost naturally gravitates to the area in which his power is greatest. The irony here, of course, is that the president has the greatest power in the area where he is potentially most dangerous and most in need of controls or checks and balances; conversely, he is most controlled in the least dangerous area, which is most in need of his leadership.

This book is about presidential weakness and the limits of power, but in the area of foreign policy, the president more closely resembles Superman, not Wimpyman. It is in the area of domestic and economic policy that the president has the most trouble getting his way.

One reason why modern presidents so often appear to fail is our tendency to judge them primarily on the basis of the success of the economy, something over which presidents have very little control. Yet, if their power is at its lowest ebb in economic policy—the area in which their reputation is most susceptible—and at its peak in the area with much less political reward, then our standards of judgment are out of whack.

This dilemma (curse?) was visited first upon George Bush, who inherited an economic mess from Ronald Reagan, and then upon Bill Clinton, whose resources and options were severely limited due to the irresponsible economic policies of the Reagan years.[258]

✪ THE SUPREME COURT

Historically, the Court has not been a very effective check on presidential power.[259] In general, the Court has supported presidential power claims and has been very hesitant to restrict the power of the president.

Under the doctrine of judicial review, the Court can exercise some control over the president. But in practice the Court has been very reluctant to get involved, and when it has, its decisions have usually expanded presidential powers, not restricted them. Especially in the areas of foreign and defense policy, the Court has been extremely reluctant to rein in the powers of the presidency.

Of course, Court decisions are like the Bible: you can find a case to support almost any conceivable position. But overall, presidency-curbing decisions by the Court have been few and far between. Can the Court serve as protector of the rule of law against presidential usurpations of power? Glendon Schubert writes that

> they [American citizens] undoubtedly expect that, should the occasion ever arise, the Supreme Court would uphold the majesty of the law against the pretensions of a usurper. History warns us, however, that this assumption may be false: in every major constitutional crisis between the executive and the judiciary, the President has emerged the victor.[260]

Schubert further notes that

> . . . the most significant aspect of judicial review of presidential orders is its ineffectiveness. If the courts are the most important bulwark of freedom and liberty in the United States, then we have every right to view with alarm the future security of the republic.[261]

The Courts have been reluctant to challenge presidential power. In fact, they have often lent judicial support to presidential power grabs. As Clinton Rossiter states, "In the nature of things judicial and political, the Court can be expected to go on rationalizing most pretensions of most presidents. It is clearly one of the least reliable restraints on presidential activity." And, "For most practical purposes, the President may act as if the Supreme Court did not exist."[262] Clearly, the president understands this. Especially in the area of foreign policy, presidents do not fear the power of the courts as a check upon their power.[263]

The concurring opinion of Justice Robert H. Jackson in the case of *Youngstown Sheet and Tube Co. v. Sawyer* (1952) provides a classic description of presidential power from the Court's perspective. Jackson posits three levels of power. In the first level, the president acts in conjunction with the expressed or implied wishes of Congress. At this level, Jackson states, the president's "authority is at its maximum." Acting together, the president and Congress are granted "the widest latitude of judicial interpretation."

The second level is, to Jackson, a "zone of twilight." Here the president and Congress share power and authority, and "congressional inertia, indifference, or quiescence may sometimes, at least as a practical matter, enable, if not invite, measures of independent presidential responsibility." Here the legitimacy of a president's actions depends on "the imperatives of the events and contemporary imponderables."

In the third level, the president is on thin constitutional ice. Here, the president engages in actions "incompatible with the expressed or implied will of Congress." In such instances, according to Jackson, the president's power is "at its lowest ebb."

Presidents prefer the logic of U.S. *v. Curtiss-Wright Export Corp.* (1936) to that of *Youngstown*. In *Curtiss-Wright*, the Supreme Court came very close to recognizing presidential omnipotence in the area of foreign affairs. Essentially, the Court decided that the federal government's powers in foreign affairs are without constitutional limitation and, further, that the executive branch exercises the foreign affairs powers, positing—in Justice Sutherland's opinion—that the president is "the sole organ of the Federal Government in the field of international relations." Clearly the Framers had something else in mind.[264]

Thus Courts allow a wide scope for presidential power *unless* the president's actions run directly against the expressed will of the Congress (the Iran-Contra scandal, for example). This gives the president considerable room to maneuver. But presidents, unsatisfied with this restriction, *claim* very expansive powers under the Constitution. President Bush went so far as to claim that he did not need a congressional declaration of support (i.e., of "war") prior to the Gulf War, but he did, in the end, seek and attain congressional approval.

Overall, the Courts have not served as a consistent or effective check on presidential power. By accepting presidential claims of inherent and implied constitutional power, the Court has accepted a rather expansive view of presidential power. Thus, in decision making, presidents rarely fear the wrath of the Court.

✪ MOVING BEYOND THE LAW

Given the numerous roadblocks and veto points that litter the president's path, it is not surprising that the more ambitious and goal-oriented presidents will get extremely frustrated as other actors block their way. An obstreperous Congress, demanding special interests, an uncooperative business community, an adversarial press, and others can at times seem to gang up on a president, preventing him from achieving his policy goals.

When faced with this myriad of opposing forces, most presidents feel caught between a rock and a hard place. Often their choice appears to be either to accept defeat or to take bold action (always, the president believes, in the national interest). To make the complex separation of powers work is difficult under the best of circumstances, and in normal times it may seem impossible to get the system moving. Thus, rather than accept defeat, some presidents are tempted to cut corners, go beyond the law, stretch the constitutional limits a bit.

When all else fails, as it often does, some presidents—knowing that their future political success, not to mention their historical reputation, is at stake—simply cannot resist going beyond the law. If the choice is gridlock or illegality, some presidents will choose the latter. After all, the president is absolutely convinced that what he wants is for the best interests of the nation, so why let a corrupt Congress, an uninformed public, or a hostile press stand in the way of progress (self-defined by the president)?

Presidents who are not well grounded in the virtues of the American system may see the system itself as the enemy and thus feel justified in going beyond the law. Richard Nixon with Watergate[265] and Ronald Reagan with the Iran-Contra scandal are but the two most pronounced examples.[266]

Sometimes a president gets away with it (e.g., Reagan); sometimes not (Nixon). But when the alternative is to stay within the law and fail (e.g., Ford, Carter), the temptation to go beyond the law—and maybe succeed and not get caught—is great, too great for some leaders to resist.

Of course, this is precisely what the Founders feared. The separation of powers and the checks and balances were set up so that ambition could counteract ambition and power could check power. The model of decision making was decidedly cooperative, not executive. But as the frustrations of high demands, high expectations, limited power, and falling approval eat away at presidents, they often cannot resist the temptation to go beyond the properly prescribed limits of the office.

Often, an attitude of arrogance overtakes the president and his top staff. "We know best" and "they are blocking progress" leads to the belief that the "slight" abuse of power is being done for the greater good. But such an attitude leads to the Imperial Presidency and its further abuses of power.[267]

The Reagan administration was absolutely convinced that communism was an evil that had to be fought at all costs, that the Marxist government in Nicaragua was a serious and direct threat to the United States, that the Congress was soft on communism, and that public opinion, which opposed U.S. intervention, was uninformed in spite of herculean efforts by the administration. Therefore, Reagan was faced with the difficult choice either to accept the will of Congress, the voice of the people, and the law or to act on his own judgment of the national interest. Reagan acted.

Putting aside the question of whether Reagan was correct about the threat Nicaragua posed to the United States, one thing is absolutely clear: the

Reagan administration decided that the law was wrong and that they would not be bound by it. This is the arrogance of power so feared by the Founders. This is a principal reason why the Founders insisted on checks and balances: to control executive tyranny and abuses of power.

The frustrations inherent in a president's inability to move the machinery of government may lead presidents to move beyond the law; they have also led scholars to articulate a more presidency-centered concept of government. In the frustrating years of Republican presidential "rule" in the 1980s, scholars on the political right—historically on the side of a more limited government and restrictions on executive power—relented to the temptation and began seeing the strong-presidency model as a tool for conservative ends. With conservatives in power but frustrated by the gridlock of the system, these scholars called for a strong president and weaker Congress.

Responding to the frustrations of Reagan's last seven years and of Bush's four years in office, writers on the political right produced calls for executive power such as Terry Eastland's *Energy in the Executive*, Corvitz and Rabkin's *The Fettered Presidency*, and Harvey C. Mansfield, Jr.'s *Taming the Prince*.[268] Gridlock, like politics itself, makes strange intellectual bedfellows.

Is the president above the law? Of course not. Such a notion violates all precepts of the rule of law.[269] But are there certain prescribed circumstances that can justify a president's going beyond the law? Are there times when the president may exceed his constitutional powers?

✪ THE PRESIDENT'S EMERGENCY POWER

When, if ever, is a president justified in stretching the Constitution? While the word *emergency* does not appear in the Constitution, there is some evidence to suggest that the Founders did envision the possibility of a president's exercising "supraconstitutional powers" in a time of national emergency.[270] The Constitution's silence, some suggest, leaves room for presidents to claim that certain constitutional provisions (e.g., Article 2, Section 1, the executive power clause, and the "faithfully execute" the law clause, along with Article 2, Section 2, the commander-in-chief clause) grant the president implied powers attendant to the performance of his job. Claims of such powers become especially pressing in times of crisis.

During a crisis, the president often assumes extra-constitutional powers.[271] The separate branches—which, under normal circumstances, are designed to check and balance a president—will usually defer to the president in times of national emergency. The president's institutional position offers him a vantage point from which he can more easily exert crisis leadership, and the Congress, Court, and public usually accept the president's judgments.

The notion of one set of legal and constitutional standards for normal conditions and another for emergency conditions raises some unsettling questions regarding democratic governments and constitutional systems.[272] Can democratic regimes function in any but prosperous, peaceful circumstances?

Or must the United States constantly rely upon the strength of a despot or "constitutional dictatorship" to save it from disaster? Are constitutional governments incapable of meeting the demands of crisis? In short, can democracy work in the twentieth century, or is it a relic of quieter times?

Democratic theory seems to be rather weak in addressing itself to the problem of crisis government and democratic objectives. In most instances, democratic political theorists have seen a need to revert to authoritarian leadership in times of crisis. Locke calls this executive "prerogative"; Rossiter refers to a "Constitutional Dictatorship"; and to Rousseau, it is an application of the "General Will." In cases of emergency, when extraordinary pressures are placed on democratic regimes, many theorists suggest that democratic systems—in order to save themselves from destruction—must defer to the ways of totalitarian regimes. In order to preserve democracy, one must, in other words, destroy democracy.

Laws decided upon by democratic means can be ignored and violated under this notion. To refer once again to Locke, in emergency situations the Crown retains the prerogative "power to act according to discretion for the public good, without the prescription of the law and sometimes even against it."[273] While this prerogative could properly be exercised only for the "public good," one cannot escape the conclusion that for democratic governments and democratic theory this is shaky ground on which to stand. And what if an executive acts wrongly? Here Locke is forced to abandon secular concerns and he writes that "the people have no other remedy in this, as in all other cases where they have no judge on earth, but to appeal to Heaven."[274]

Rousseau likewise recognized the need for a temporary suspension of democratic procedures in times of crisis. In the *Social Contract* he notes:

> The inflexibility of the laws, which prevents them from adapting themselves to circumstances, may, in certain cases, render them disastrous, and make them bring about a time of crisis, the ruin of the State.
>   . . . If . . . the peril is of such a kind that the paraphernalia of the laws are an obstacle to their preservation, the method is to nominate a supreme ruler, who shall silence all the laws and suspend for a moment the sovereign authority. In such a case, there is no doubt about the general will, and it is clear that the people's first intention is that the State shall not perish.[275]

The major difference between Locke and Rousseau on this matter rests in Rousseau's refusal to rely upon an "appeal to Heaven" in cases of possible abuse of the power of the "supreme magistracy." Rousseau emphasized that this power must have strictly enforced time limitations as a protection against a complete takeover of the system. But once extraordinary power is assumed by one individual ruler, who can be sure that such time limits can and will be adhered to?

John Stuart Mill, after defending representative government, makes this "uncharacteristic" comment: "I am far from condemning, in cases of extreme necessity, the assumption of absolute power in the form of a temporary dictatorship."[276]

Smith and Cotter sum up this problem in the writings of democratic theorists when they note that

> democratic political theorists tacitly admit the existence of a fatal defect in any system of constitutional democracy: Its processes are inadequate to confront and overcome emergency.[277]

And Niccolò Machiavelli, no great "democrat" himself, addresses this problem when he notes that

> in a well-ordered republic it should never be necessary to resort to extra-constitutional measures; for although they may for the time be beneficial, yet the precedent is pernicious, for if the practice is once established of disregarding the laws for good objects, they will in a little while be disregarded under that pretext for evil purposes. Thus no republic will ever be perfect if she has not by law provided for everything, having a remedy for every emergency, and fixed rules for applying it.[278]

Clinton Rossiter's "Constitutional Dictatorship" is a modern version of the same problem that democratic theorists attempted (unsuccessfully, I suggest) to solve.[279] The "Constitutional Dictatorship" is an admission of the weakness of democratic theory, or of its failure to cover the full range of governing requirements. To save democracy, we escape from it. To protect democracy, we reject it. Democratic theory then, according to the democratic theorists, is incomplete; in cases of emergency, one is called upon to reject democracy for the more expedient ways of the dictator. In this manner, democratic theory opens the door to a strong, power-aggrandizing executive.

Nowhere in the Constitution is it specified that the president will have additional powers in times of crisis or emergency. But history has shown us that in times of national emergency, the powers of the president have greatly expanded, and while Abe Fortas writes that "Under the Constitution, the President has no implied powers which enable him to make or disregard laws,"[280] under the microscope of political reality we can see that this is precisely what American presidents have done.

The outcome of this view of an enlarged reservoir of presidential power in emergencies has been characterized by Edward S. Corwin as "constitutional relativity."[281] Corwin's view finds the Constitution broad and flexible enough to meet the needs of an emergency situation as defined and measured by its own provisions. By this approach, the Constitution can be adapted, in short, to meet the needs of the times. If the times call for quasi-dictatorial action by the executive, the Court could find this acceptable.

The problem of emergency situations in democratic systems is not easily answered. If the potential power of the state is used too little or too late, the democratic state faces the possibility of destruction. If used arbitrarily and capriciously, this power could lead the system to accept a form of permanent dictatorship. In a contemporary sense, the constant reliance on the executive to solve the many "emergencies" (self-defined by the executive) facing America could very well lead to the acceptance of the overly powerful executive and make the meaning of the term "emergency" shallow and susceptible to executive manipulation.

With each new "emergency" in American history, the public and our political institutions seemed to become more accustomed to accepting a broader definition of presidential power to meet each new crisis. In the twentieth century, it seems hardly a debatable point to say that a president is expected to assume responsibility and added powers to meet both domestic and foreign crises.

The Court under Rossiter's constitutional dictatorship will generally recognize the need for the government to have inflated powers with which to deal with the impending crisis, and it will allow for a "flexible" interpretation of the constitutional powers of the president, who is usually expected to deal with the emergency. For as Rossiter notes:

> In the last resort, it is always the executive branch in the government which possesses and wields the extraordinary powers of self-preservation of any democratic, constitutional state.[282]

The Court, under Rossiter's theory, recognizes the emergency and allows the president to assume additional powers. But the constitutional dictator must recognize the limits of his responsibilities. Franklin D. Roosevelt, in 1942, after claiming/requesting of Congress a grant of an unusually large amount of power, assured the legislature that "When the war is won, the powers under which I act automatically revert to the people—to whom they belong."[283] The executive, in short, will return the extraordinary powers he was granted during the crisis back to their rightful place. But serious questions remain as to (1) whether presidents have in fact returned this power, and (2) whether, even if the president desired to do so, a complete or even reasonable return to normality is possible after dictatorial or quasi-dictatorial power is placed in the hands of one man. In sum, can a democracy survive without a strong executive, and conversely, can a democracy exist with one?

Recognizing the need for expanded presidential power in order to meet the necessities of emergencies, political scientist Richard M. Pious attempts to distinguish between the legitimate and illegitimate use of emergency power by a president. Pious refers to seven "standards of behavior" that clarify this distinction:

1. The exercise of power should not involve personal or partisan advantage, nor should it interfere with the constitutional processes of election or succession to office.

2. The powers must be exercised in a national emergency, when the continued existence of the Union and the physical safety of the people is at stake, when delay might prove fatal, and when traditional constitutional procedures would involve such delay.

3. The powers are exercised when no statute or precedent provides a viable alternative procedure, and nothing in the Constitution or laws of the land expressly prohibit the actions.

4. Use of prerogative powers should be preceded by the widest possible consultation within the government, including senior officials in the departments, and when possible, leaders of Congress. The president should try to create a consensus that emergency government must be instituted.

5. The president should make available to Congress and the judiciary a full record involving his actions as soon as practicable during or after the emergency. Courts should make the final determination if he claims executive privilege.

6. Once the emergency has passed Congress should legislate to routinize procedures, placing powers on a statutory basis, and should provide for legislative and judicial review if appropriate.

7. The checks and balances system must function throughout the emergency, permitting possible resolutions of censure or an impeachment proceeding.[284]

✪ PRESIDENTIAL ACTION IN TIMES OF EMERGENCY

History has shown us that the President's emergency power has indeed been great in comparison to his powers under normal circumstances. When faced with a crisis situation, presidents have made exaggerated claims of power, have acted upon these claims, and generally have gotten away with these excessive, and often extralegal, uses of power. History indeed provides us with clear examples of the enormous power of a president in an emergency situation.

The American political system has met crises with an expansion of presidential power. In emergency periods, the president may act with little regard for the wishes and dictates of the other branches. While the Constitution does not refer to any additional powers for the president during emergencies, the political reality has shown us that in times of crisis, the president becomes the prime mover of the American system. The necessity for quick, decisive, often extra-constitutional actions that the crisis may demand, places a heavy burden upon the president. Since he is the only leader able to move quickly, the burden of meeting the crisis "must" fall on his shoulders. According to Richard Longaker, "In time of crisis constitutional limitations bend to other needs."[285]

Lincoln during the Civil War and Franklin Roosevelt during the depression serve as examples of presidents who, when faced with a crisis, acted boldly, assumed power, became constitutional dictators.[286] But what distinguishes the constitutional dictator from the Imperial President? What separates the actions of Lincoln and Roosevelt, generally considered to be appropriate, from those of Nixon and Reagan, generally considered inappropriate or imperial?

Essentially, for the crisis presidency to be valid, (1) the president must face a genuine and a widely recognized emergency; (2) the Congress and public must—more or less—accept that the president will exercise supra-constitutional powers; (3) the Congress *may*, if it chooses, override presidential acts; (4) the president's acts must be public so as to allow Congress and the public to judge them; (5) there must be no suspension of the next election; and (6) the president should consult with Congress where possible (see Pious's list in the previous section). We can see that Lincoln and Roosevelt met (more or less) all of these requirements; Nixon and Reagan, very few of them.

Even when the requirements are met, however, one should not be sanguine about presidential usurpations of power. As the Supreme Court reminded us in Ex *parte Milligan* (4 Wall. 2, 1866): "Wicked men, ambitious of power, with a hatred of liberty and contempt of law, may fill the place once occupied by Washington and Lincoln."

❂ CONCLUSION

Presidential leadership (true leadership as opposed to mere office holding) is a rare commodity. In those rare moments of leadership, presidents were able to animate citizens and mobilize government, develop a vision and establish an agenda, move the Congress and push the bureaucracy. Such presidents recast the arena of the politically possible. It hasn't happened often. The forces arrayed against a president usually have the upper hand. The power of lethargy is truly daunting.

The preconditions for effective presidential leadership are so rarely in syncopation: skill, the right timing, a consensus, a governing coalition, high popularity, vision, a clear mandate, and so forth. Presidents, to be effective leaders in a democratic system, must bring Hamiltonian energy, to a Madisonian system, for Jeffersonian ends. Lamentably, most presidents fail in this task.

For a leader to be effective, he needs the vision of John Kennedy, the political skills of Lyndon Johnson, the strategic insight of Richard Nixon, the genuineness of Gerald Ford, the character of Jimmy Carter, the charisma of Ronald Reagan, the experience of George Bush, and the interpersonal skills (and wife) of Bill Clinton. It also helps, as Machiavelli reminds us, to have *fortuna* on our side.

This chapter has presented the building blocks of presidential leadership. Even so, how a president puts these blocks together—his strategic sense—tells only part of the story. For a president to succeed, he needs to have both a good strategic or power sense and also the benefit of circumstances or conditions (opportunities) that lend themselves to presidential leadership. The preconditions of power are of equal or greater than equal importance to skill in achieving success.

To succeed, presidents must be masters of the *light* (education, vision, mobilization) and the *heat* (power, bargaining). Given the incredible array of skills and circumstances necessary for presidents to succeed, it is no wonder that most of them either fail or at best give mediocre performances.

✪ FOR DISCUSSION

1. Can we really expect presidents to lead in domestic policy in normal (non-crisis) times? In normal times, does the president have sufficient resources to govern?

2. How can we (and should we) give the president more power in domestic affairs and less power in foreign affairs and war?

3. Do we overload the president? How can any president "do it all"?

4. Given that the presidency is an impossible job, what sorts of experiences or training best prepare someone for the office?

✪ DEBATE QUESTIONS

I. Resolved: That presidents have become slaves to public opinion polls and rarely exercise leadership.

II. Resolved: That the media, rather than serving as a check on the executive, are easily manipulated by presidents.

Chapter 4

★★

MAKING THE PRESIDENCY EFFECTIVE *AND* ACCOUNTABLE

Still the question recurs "can we do better?" The dogmas of the quiet past, are inadequate to the stormy present. The occasion is piled high with difficulty, and we must rise with the occasion. As our case is new, so we *must think anew, and act anew.*

—Abraham Lincoln, Annual Message to Congress, December 1, 1862

A decade ago, Harold Barger began the concluding chapter of his book *The Impossible Presidency* with the following:

> Has the presidency become chronically unstable, or is it only suffering from a temporary downturn not unlike earlier cycles in which Congress dominated the Executive Branch? Is the decline of the office due to a succession of less qualified chief executives, or has the presidency become imperiled by a host of political and social problems at home and abroad that defy solutions? Can any president serve out a full term and still look forward to reelection, or is there no longer much hope that there is "life after inauguration"?
>
> Deep misgivings about the presidency have surfaced during the past five administrations, paralleling a growing frustration and loss of confidence that have marked our nation at least since Vietnam and Watergate. A yearning for strong national leadership has long since extinguished fears about an imperial president. For Americans now seem to be less concerned about presidential abuse of power than they are by the inability of presidents to wield power at all.
>
> Thoughtful observers of our politics grow uneasy over the chronic inability of the United States to develop stable, coherent policies to deal with domestic problems and global dangers. Chaotic swings in the political fortunes of one president after another raise serious questions as to whether *anyone* can manage the U.S. store. An increasing number of political experts now wonder if the office can ever function with reasonable efficiency *without* major reforms in the selection process and in the Constitutional powers of the presidency.[287]

It is amazing that a decade later those words sound as fresh as if they had been written this morning.

Having established (Chapter 1) that the presidents of the past twenty-five years have been inadequate to the task of governing; and having discussed

(Chapter 2) the primary reasons why presidents usually fail; and further, having discussed (Chapter 3) how presidents, under certain circumstances, can overcome the anti-leadership tendencies built into the American system, it is now time to turn our attention to a broader, perhaps more difficult question: What do we want of our presidents?

Is the current, inhibited state of presidential power/leadership acceptable, or do we want to trade in the eighteenth-century Constitution for a newer, more streamlined model, one perhaps better suited to the demands of the twentieth and twenty-first centuries?

Americans have historically had a difficult time deciding what it wanted of its leaders: someone to pull us forward, or someone to follow our wishes; someone to act forcefully, or someone to execute the people's will. Likewise, Americans have historically had a difficult time reconciling leadership with our democratic aspirations. Having said this, it is equally (though no less problematically) true that "American political thought has not lacked admirers of leadership."[288]

Because of our ambivalence and confusion regarding the proper range and scope of powers to be invested in the presidency, we swing back and forth between the desire for heroic leaders to "save" us and the desire to contain, if not destroy, the leaders who disappoint us. The pendulum swings back and forth between eras when we invest too much hope in leaders and eras of disposable leaders and the dwarfing of the presidency. As Burns has noted, "We search eagerly for leadership yet seek to cage and tame it."[289] But "power," if it be exercised wisely and in the interests of the people, cannot be so harnessed nor so liberated as to make it either ineffectual or dangerous.

Just what do we want of the presidency? Part of the difficulty inherent in such a question stems from a historical dilemma: the Founders themselves were never quite clear as to what they wanted of the institution. Constitutionally they left the presidency vague and unformed, hoping that the venerated George Washington would set appropriate precedents.[290] But how well do eighteenth-century precedents work as we approach the twenty-first century? Perhaps it is time, in the spirit of Jefferson, who believed that no generation should be enslaved by the dogmas of the past, to ask anew: what do we want of the U.S. presidency? As Jefferson himself noted:

> Some men look at constitutions with sanctimonious reverence and deem them like the ark of the covenant, too sacred to be touched. They ascribe to the men of the preceding age a wisdom more than human, and suppose what they did to be beyond amendment. I knew that age well; I belonged to it, and labored with it. It deserved well of its country. It was very like the present, but without the experience of the present; and forty years of experience in government is worth a century of bookreading; and this they would say themselves, were they to rise from the dead. . . . Institutions must advance also, and keep pace with the times. We might as well require a man to wear still the coat which fitted him when a boy. . . .[291]

There is yet another compelling reason to reexamine the scope of presidential power: the end of the Cold War. In the Cold War era (1945–1989), it was widely believed that the United States, as the hegemonic power of the West, required strong presidential leadership (especially in foreign affairs).[292] But with the collapse of the Soviet empire, we are free from "some" of the burden of power imposed by the dangers of the Cold War. Freed of the weight of the Cold War we can ask: In the post–Cold War world, what powers and limits do we wish to invest in the presidency in this "post-hegemonic era"?[293]

Put another way, as we approach the next century and the new world before us, we must find out "how to empower the president without endangering the system."[294] While the president's formal powers are rather limited, his informal powers may help to overcome the limits of the office, but skill can only go so far. And, paradoxically, there are areas in which the president clearly has too little power (domestic and economic policy) and simultaneously areas where he has too much power (foreign policy and war).

Our confusion is complicated by the fact that leadership often seems at odds with democracy. We know leadership is important, but can we truly reconcile our need for leadership with our belief in democracy? Thomas E. Cronin believes we must.

> The challenge, for those who care about our nation and the dreams of constitutional democracy, is to seek ways to reconcile these concepts—leadership and democracy. Whether we like it or not, our democracy will stand or fall on the quality of leaders as well as on the quality of citizens we produce and nurture here.[295]

And Cronin attempts to provide guidance in how we can democratize leadership by calling for a rebirth of citizen politics. As he writes,

> The challenge of reconciling leadership and democracy is part definitional, part attitudinal, and part behavioral. We have too long held a view of leaders that is hierarchical, male, and upon which followers, like subjects or slaves, are dependent. That conception is antithetical to our democratic aspirations. The very word "followers" is a negative and demeaning word and ought, if possible, to be discarded or at least greatly modified. For a nation of subservient followers can never be a democratic one. A democratic nation requires educated, skeptical, caring, engaged, and contentious citizen-leaders—citizens who are willing to lead as well as follow, who are willing to point the way as often as they are persuaded in one way or another, and prize the spirit of liberty and free speech that animates our Bill of Rights.[296]

Only by creating a cadre of citizen-leaders can we hope to democratize (and thereby empower) leadership in the United States. But is this possible in the fractious, divisive, and petty politics of left versus right?

Presidents who lead in the democratic spirit create leaders, foster citizen responsibility, inspire and empower others to assume leadership responsibilities in their communities. Democratic leaders establish a moral vision; pursue egalitarian goals; question, challenge, engage, and educate citizens; offer hope. Emiliano Zapata said that "strong leaders make a weak people."[297] But *strong democratic leaders* help create *strong citizens*. Eugene Debs captured the dilemma when he said: "Too long have the workers of the world waited for some Moses to lead them out of bondage. He has not come; he will not come.

I would not lead you out if I could; for if you would be led out, you could be led back again."[298]

✪ JEFFERSON'S VISION OF DEMOCRATIC LEADERSHIP[299]

Democratic theorists have long wrestled with a particularly vexing question: Is there such a thing as "Democratic Leadership" or are the two words mutually exclusive if not contradictory? Thomas E. Cronin has gone so far as to call them "warring concepts."[300] But can any system of government exist without leadership? For those who believe in the superiority of democracy over other forms of government, a way must be found to reconcile these two seemingly warring concepts into a sustainable whole.

The tension between the need for leadership and the demands of democracy was reinforced by James Bryce, who reminded us that "perhaps no form of government needs great leaders so much as democracy."[301] But what kind of leadership? The strong, forceful direction of a heroic leader, or the gentle guiding hand of a teacher?

Proponents of robust democracy realize, as Bruce Miroff has written, that

> leadership has rarely fit comfortably with democracy in America. The claim of leaders to political precedence violates the equality of democratic citizens. The most committed democrats have been suspicious of the very idea of leadership. When Thomas Paine railed against the "slavish custom of following leaders, he expressed a democrat's deepest anxiety."[302]

But such tensions have not prevented Americans from looking to strong leaders to guide the republic. Especially during a crisis, we turn to our leaders in hopes that strong or heroic leadership can save the republic. Thus, while we are suspicious of strong leadership, we also admire it. As Arthur M. Schlesinger, Jr., has noted,

> The American democracy has readily resorted in practice to the very leadership it had disclaimed in theory. An adequate democratic theory must recognize that democracy is not self-executing: that leadership is not the enemy of self-government but the means of making it work; that followers have their own stern obligation, which is to keep leaders within rigorous constitutional bounds; and that Caesarism is more often produced by the failure of feeble governments than by the success of energetic ones.[303]

Dilemmas notwithstanding, is there a style of leadership compatible with political democracy? While a tension will always exist between leadership and democracy, there are ways to bring the two into a creative tension that both calls for a role for the leader and also promotes democratic participation and practices among the citizenry.

Just as Abraham Lincoln gave us a succinct, eloquent definition of democracy as "government of the people, by the people, for the people,"[304] so too did one of America's other Mt. Rushmore leaders give us an eloquent, even simple definition of democratic leadership. Thomas Jefferson believed that the primary duties of a leader in a democracy were *"to inform the minds of the people, and to follow their will"*[305] (emphasis added).

There are two key concepts contained in Jefferson's brief definition: *inform minds*, and *follow the people's will*. Informing the minds of the people speaks to the role of leader as educator. In a democracy, the leader has a responsibility to educate, enlighten, and inform the people. He or she must identify problems and mobilize the people to act. By informing or educating the citizenry, the leader also engages in a dialogue, the ultimate goal of which is to involve leader and citizen in the process of developing a vision, grounded in the values of the nation, which will animate future action.

The leader's task in a democracy is to look ahead, see problems, focus the public's attention on the work that must be done, provide alternative courses of action, chart a path for the future, and move the nation in support of his or her ideas. The leader must attempt to mobilize the public around a vision and secure a consensus on the proper way to proceed.

The second component of Jefferson's definition, to "follow their will," suggests that after educating and involving the people, the leader must ultimately follow the will of the people. Several commentators have noted the distinction between the whim of the people (temporary and changing) and the will of the people (deeply held truths that speak to the nation's highest aspirations). The leader's job is to inform, educate, and persuade the public to embrace and work for a vision that taps into the deeper truths and higher purposes of the will of Americans. But whatever their judgment, the leader must serve the people and ultimately follow their direction.

In a democracy, following the will of the people is essential. Any leader who pursues policies contrary to the expressed wishes of the people can be accused of the democratic cardinal sin: defying the will of the people. Thus, to be a leader requires, first, that one use all possible means to bring about informed judgments by the people. Then, the leader must *serve* the people. This form of democratic accountability calls for the leader to play an important role, but it ultimately relies upon the people to make final judgments.

In this sense, Ronald Reagan did not exercise democratic leadership in the case of Nicaragua. Reagan believed that the Sandinistas, who controlled Nicaragua, were a threat to U.S. interests. He attempted to enlighten the public on this issue but failed to change public opinion. Congress, in line with public opinion, passed restrictive legislation, banning U.S. assistance to the rebels (Contras) who were attempting to overthrow the Nicaraguan government. In spite of this, the Reagan administration violated both the law and the public's wish, and assisted the Contras. This is the type of leadership that the Founders feared and that contradicts democratic standards.

The best democratic leadership, in Bruce Miroff's words, "not only serves people's interests but furthers their democratic dignity as well."[306] Thus, Thomas Jefferson's vision of a democratic leadership that informs the public, then follows their will, elevates both leader and citizen. Such a form of leadership is difficult, time consuming, and fraught with pitfalls. But it is a style of leadership that builds strong citizens for a strong democracy.

✪ A POWERFUL *AND* ACCOUNTABLE PRESIDENT?

Can the presidency be made powerful *and* accountable? Can the president lead but not become an autocrat?

In some areas—foreign policy and war, for example—the president has perhaps too much power. In other areas, domestic and economic policy, the president seems too weak. The former means we often get heroic but undemocratic leadership; the latter means we often lead presidential lambs to political slaughter. Overall, the "system" of presidential leadership is dysfunctional. Presidents do not build coalitions, they do not generate consensus, and they sometimes act as independent policy entrepreneurs. This is not democratic leadership. It is not leadership.

In the beginning of this book, I offered a "theory" of presidential politics: *Presidents, facing a system of multiple veto points, seek to maximize power and influence.* How well, or poorly, does this theory explain presidential behavior? I fear that while it may capture the core of presidential behavior, there are still loose ends that remain unexplained. Presidential scholars have long bemoaned the absence of theory in the study of the presidency,[307] and this may be a function both of the complexity and the many-sidedness of the institution. Can we find "a" theory that truly explains presidential behavior, or must we move from president to president, trying to explain why *that one individual* succeeded or failed? I have argued that while individual presidents vary in skill, style, ideology, and other ways, they are also a part of ongoing and recurrent patterns of behavior that shape the *presidency.* Thus, while any theory of presidential behavior will fall short of explaining every act by every individual president (which is not the job of a theory), a good theory captures the core, the essence of its subject. I hope that such a task was fulfilled by this theory of presidential behavior.

The United States needs a strong presidency and a democratically controlled presidency, a strong presidency and *strong citizenship.*[308] Benjamin R. Barber notes the difficulty inherent in such a hope:

> At the heart of democratic theory lies a profound dilemma that has afflicted democratic practice at least since the eighteenth century. Democracy requires both effective leadership and vigorous citizenship: yet the conditions and consequences of leadership often seem to undermine civic vigor. Although it cries for both, democracy must customarily make do either with strong leadership or with strong citizens. For the most part, depending on devices of representation in large-scale societies, democracy in the West has settled for strong leaders and correspondingly weak citizens.[309]

James Madison's caution in *The Federalist*, no. 51, speaks volumes in today's world:

> If men were angels, no government would be necessary. If angels were to govern man, neither external nor internal controls in government would be necessary. In framing a government which is to be administered by men over men the great difficulty lies in this, you must first enable the government to control the governed and in the next place oblige it to control itself. A dependence on the people is no doubt the primary control on the government. But experience has taught mankind the necessity for auxiliary precautions.

How can one give power but control it? Can the presidency be empowered but democratized?

Of course, our desire for strong presidential leadership seems contrary to the goal of holding presidents accountable. Leadership implies power; accountability implies limits. Contradictions aside, accountability is a fundamental piece of the democratic puzzle. In essence it denotes that public officials are answerable for their actions. But to whom? Within what limits? Through what means?

There are three types of accountability: *ultimate accountability* (which the United States has via the impeachment process); *periodic accountability* (provided for by general elections); and *daily accountability* (somewhat contained in the separation of powers).[310] James Madison believed that elections provided the "primary check on government" and that the separation of powers ("ambition will be made to counteract ambition") plus "auxiliary precautions" would take care of the rest.[311]

Of course, there *are* times when presidents abuse power or behave corruptly.[312] But even in the two most recent bouts with presidential abuses, Watergate and the Iran-Contra scandal, the president was stopped by the countervailing forces of a free press, an independent Congress, an independent judiciary, and (belatedly) an aroused public.

Presidents can be held accountable, but can they be held responsible? That is, can they muster enough power to govern? One means to improve accountability and also empower leadership is to strengthen the party system in America. Our parties are—at least by European standards—weak, undisciplined, and nonideological. A stronger party system could organize and mobilize citizens and government, diminish the fragmentation of the separation of powers, and mitigate against the atomization of our citizenry. If the parties were more disciplined and programmatic, the government's ability to govern could be greatly enhanced.

A more responsible party system would also ground presidents in a more consensus-oriented style of leadership, and thereby diminish the independent, unconnected brand of leadership so often attempted by recent presidents. A stronger party system would be one way to help make the separation of powers work better. At present the institutional relation between the president and Congress is too often characterized as conflict if not combat. What is needed is cooperation. A more robust party system can help join the president and Congress together in a more cooperative relationship.[313]

✪ THE ENDS AND MEANS OF PRESIDENTIAL POWER

All presidents want to be successful, but what does it mean to be a success? High popularity? A good historical reputation? Achieving one's policy goals? A high congressional box score? Getting one's way?

If success is measured merely by getting one's way, then many bullies are successful. But success in leadership means more than getting what one wants. In determining success, we must always ask "power for what *ends*?" because power divorced from purpose is potentially dangerous and democratically undesirable.

In a democracy, people tend to get the government they deserve. If we look upon government as the enemy, and politics as a dirty word, our anger turns to apathy, allowing power (but not responsibility) to slip through our hands; we look at politics not as a means to achieve public good, but as a necessary evil; we see elections as the choice between the lesser of two evils or the evil of two lessers; we presume that our democratic responsibilities are satisfied merely by the act of voting every so often, or we drop out of politics. In short, if we abandon politics, power abandons us. So we return to a question asked earlier in this book: How do we bring Hamiltonian energy to the Madisonian system to achieve Jeffersonian ends?[314] If democracies have trouble finding and supporting leaders who seek to democratize power, they have an equally difficult time measuring success. While there is no easily computed presidential batting average to measure success, Emerson, answering the question "What is success?" came close:

> To laugh often and love much, to win the respect of intelligent persons and the affection of children; to appreciate beauty; to find the best in others; to give one's self; to leave the world a lot better whether by a healthy child, a garden patch, or a redeemed social condition; to have played and laughed with enthusiasm and sung with exaltation, to know even one life has breathed easier because you have lived—this is to have succeeded.[315]

In a *democracy*, a *successful leader* pursues and uses power, not for selfish ends, not to aggrandize his or her own status, but to achieve the goals of *empowerment*. Democratic leaders are *educators*, they are *visionaries*. They move the government in pursuit of the consensus generated from the values of the nation. They appeal to the best in citizens and attempt to lead the nation toward its better self.[316]

Franklin Roosevelt reminded us that the presidency "is preeminently a place of moral leadership."[317] Thus, presidents may use their office as a "bully pulpit" to—when at their best—lead democratically. While the current cynicism and disdain about government sweeps the land—partly the result, I have argued, of the persistence of failed presidencies—let us not forget the great good to which government can and has been used. After all, it was through politics and government that the great social movements of this century helped move us toward greater racial and gender equality, devised policies to expand education and opportunities to a wider segment of the population, attempted to protect and expand the rights of citizens. These battles are far from over. As a nation, we have a long way to go before we can truly grant the blessings of liberty and prosperity on all our fellow citizens, but it is through politics—and only through politics—that we can hope to achieve these noble goals. And if we want our politics (our government) to succeed, we must find ways for citizen power to guide, ennoble, and empower presidential leadership.

The ends that power serves are important, but in presidential terms, virtue is not enough. A successful president must have *character* and *competence*. Character without competence (resources, skill, power) gives us noble but ineffective leaders; competence without character may lead to government by demagogues.

✪ SEPARATION OR SYNCOPATION?

In theory, the separation of powers diminishes the chances of tyranny and increases the need for consensus and cooperation. In practice, there may very well be too much separation and too little power to act.[318]

In thinking about how to reform the presidency, the U.S. system of separating power is often compared with the British parliamentary model of the *fusion of* power. The British system brings the prime minister and Parliament together; it unifies power under a system of cabinet or prime ministerial rule in a strong-party model. The party in power selects the prime minister, who then has a considerable amount of power to achieve his or her policy goals.[319]

Most people (even most scholars) are comfortable with the idea of strong presidential leadership. On the left and right, the heroic-presidency model has begun to dominate the literature on presidential power. But what kind of strong presidency? One based on the Gaullist model? A presidency unhinged from the separation of powers?

As a gross overgeneralization, one could say that, historically, the political left has been more favorably disposed to the strong-presidency model, and the political right has been suspicious of a strong presidency. This reflected the old (outdated?) split between liberals and conservatives, with liberals inclined to use the power of the federal government to achieve liberal ends (the FDR model), and conservatives more inclined to rely on the "magic of the free market" to achieve social and economic goals.

But after years and years of failed or divided governments, a convergence has occurred. Today, all sides are drawn to the strong-presidency model. On the left, for example, former Carter administration official Lloyd Cutler calls for a parliamentary reform agenda, as do a number of academicians.[320]

What is surprising (and a historical anomaly) is that today, the political right embraces the strong-presidency model. Encouraged by the early days of Reagan's first term, conservatives began to believe that the heroic presidency model could serve conservative ends. Conservative activists like Terry Eastland, academics like Jeremy Rabkin, and political philosophers like Harvey Mansfield, Jr.,[321] all see the activist presidency as a conservative change agent worthy of support.

It seems that today the only place one can find defenses of the separation of powers, of the Framers' model, is in the academy. Scholars such as Tom Cronin, Robert Spitzer, and Harold Koh[322] eloquently defend the legitimacy of the Founders' vision, arguing that our system is, after all, a tale of three branches, not one. But they sometimes seem to be driving against traffic.

✪ REFORMING THE PRESIDENCY

The American presidency, while the subject of much criticism and disappointment, has lasted for over two hundred years. The system created by Madison

"*Well, guess I did it again eh guys? Missed a field goal in the final seconds. But, hey, we're a team, right? . . . Guys?*"

and the other Founders has lasted more or less intact for an amazingly long time by comparative standards. It is thus time to pay tribute to the Framers, but it is also time to honor their memory by reexamining the institution of the presidency and ask: Is this the best we can do? Is this eighteenth-century document adequate for governing in the twentieth and, soon, the twenty-first century?

The Framers would most certainly have been pleased to see how the system of checks and balances has thwarted executive tyranny. But they would perhaps have been less pleased with the excessive gridlock that so often characterizes relations between the president and Congress. The Founders wanted to limit presidential power, not spay and neuter the office.

"How," Bert Rockman asks in *The Leadership Question*, "can leadership be exerted yet restrained?"[323] It is a question that confounded the Founders and troubles us today.

Is the separation-of-powers model *the* problem? Does it create a magical gridlock machine? If one is the president, there must be times when it seems so. Woodrow Wilson—writing in 1884 *before* occupying the White House—saw the separation as creating a massive political escape clause for blame and responsibility:

> Power and strict accountability for its use are the essential constituents of good government. . . . It is, therefore, manifestly a radical defect in our federal system that it parcels out power and confuses responsibility as it does. The main purpose of the Convention of 1787 seems to have been to accomplish this grievous mistake. . . . Were it possible to call together again the members of that wonderful Convention . . . they would be the first to admit that the only fruit of dividing power had been to make it irresponsible.[324]

But upon reflection we are reminded of the positive benefit of separating, sharing, and overlapping power. If one values deliberation, discussion, and debate; if we accept a model of democratic governing based on consensus and cooperation, then the reform agenda will be short. But many see the separation as the likely suspect in the crime of gridlock.

Among reformers, there is a great deal of sympathy for the parliamentary alternative, but it must be admitted that with the American reverence for the Constitution, to make such a dramatic change is out of the question. Even if parliamentary reform were the panacea that some of its proponents suggest, there is simply no way to expect the American people to pursue such a radical restructuring of their system of government.

The choice, then, is not between radical restructuring *or* tinkering; not between dealing with root causes *or* symptoms; not between major surgery *or* an aspirin. The only choice we face, given the sacredness of the constitutional order, is to ask, Which form of tinkering *might* make the system operate a bit better? Which Band-Aids might bring just a bit more fusion to a system so separated? While there is no surefire antidote to presidential failure, there *must* be a way to make the system operate better than its current performance levels.

✪ MAKING THE PRESIDENCY WORK!

To make the presidency work, to make it powerful but accountable, to help the presidency serve Jeffersonian ends, we must focus our attention widely on more than a single institution. The presidency does not exist in a vacuum, and presidential reforms, as important as they may be, cannot be instituted in isolation of the other important elements of the political system.

We must change the presidency, but *we* must change also. We must make the presidency work, but we must also reform Congress, change public expectations and demands, reform the party system, and more. Given the interconnectedness of the American system, not the reform of one branch but the reform of the American governmental system should be our goal. It is, after all, a tale of three branches, not one. And while ours is a presidentially driven system (Congress leads only rarely[325]), it is also a system driven by cooperation and engagement between the separate institutions that share power.

First and foremost, we must accept the legitimacy of the separation of powers and the theory of government (consensus-building, cooperative) that rests behind it. Presidents and Congress must find reasons and ways to *work together*, lest they continue to face the deadlock and gridlock that has plagued recent years.[326] But can we make the separation of powers work better so that separation does not mean isolation? Can the president and Congress cooperate, or are they cursed to perpetually exhibit the most dysfunctional side of their separation?

The first precondition of making the separation of powers work better is the need to develop a *consensus*. This does not mean that all Americans must march in lockstep behind the will of the majority, but it does point to the need for Americans to feel like a nation once again: a people joined together in common pursuit of the common good—a nation, not merely an aggregation of individuals. The current division between Congress and the president reflects not merely the institutional battles between two branches of government but also the deeper conflicts and divisions that divide the nation and its people.

The only way to achieve a consensus is to begin a nationwide discussion, a dialogue of self-examination. We must ask: Who are we (as a people)? What do we want? Where do we wish to go? How can we get there?

If we are a people divided by race, class, religion, or ideology, we must find ways to move beyond the balkanization of cultures and develop a shared sense of national community. The end of the Cold War, rather than producing a sense of euphoria, has revealed a state of national confusion. Our national purpose, which seemed so clear in the Cold War era, is now characterized by self-doubt and drift. Gone is the road map that guided us. In its place is the void. We have no useful interpretative framework to replace the Cold War consensus that so dominated the American psyche. We are left with a crisis of modernity in which the search for meaning has led to confusion.

We can continue to drift aimlessly from one election to another, one party to another, one candidate to another, or we can engage in a dialogue focused on the search for the meaning of national community in a post–Cold War world.[327] Most "leaders" fear the consequences of such a discussion. But the leader who can master this dilemma, the party that can mobilize the voters behind such a vision, will create the conditions for the next critical realignment of the American political system. Critical realignments give direction and meaning to the task of governing. Out of critical realignments comes the consensus that facilitates leadership.

We are a diverse nation, a complex nation, a multicultural nation, a heterogeneous nation. Can we truly get along? Can we become, once again, a nation? Can we pull together for the common good and the general welfare?

If we are to move ahead as a nation, we cannot rely simply on leaders taking us in new directions. Reform must percolate up as a result of national renewal and reinvention. Can we reinvent democracy and reinvent government for the public good?[328]

A rebirth of citizen democracy, to use Tom Cronin's phrase, is needed if we are to recapture the lost essence of Jeffersonian democracy. Not the negative, hurtful activism that tears down the nation, but a hopeful, helpful, positive spirit of community and unity. For too long have we been at each other's throats; for too long have we been more inclined to tear down than to build up. Both the left and the right share in the blame for this "politics of contempt." In the late 1960s, many on the left misunderstood liberty to mean license, and freedom to mean free from responsibility. The right of today are currently engaged in their own version of "trash America." With their celebration of greed and the condemnation of diversity, they flock to the cynicism of a Rush Limbaugh and are made to feel temporarily better by mocking America (always under the guise of Americanism). In the right's current rush to Limbaugh (as opposed to a rush to limbo—the latter requiring a great deal of flexibility; the former requiring absolute rigidity), it seeks to make political advantage out of mocking America. As the cynicism of the 1960s could not last, so too will the cynicism of the 1980s and 1990s wear thin after a time.

To replace the cynicism that has torn us apart, we need a sense of national identify that can bring us together. The needs of individualism (1980s) and community (1960s) must be brought into balance. As citizens we must lower our political expectations and increase our political knowledge; we must embrace our diversity and build on our dreams. We must become a nation again.

A great deal needs to be done in Congress (to Congress?) to reinvent the separation of powers for the twenty-first century. The system in which the Congress holds the president hostage or the system in which the president circumvents Congress must end. To make the separation of powers work better (as intended?), the Congress needs to (a) strengthen party leadership within Congress; (b) strengthen the parties (this wouldn't be a political science book without a call for stronger parties); (c) greatly diminish the importance of money in the congressional and political process; and (d) institute a form of the British model of "Question Time," in which the president appears before Congress to answer questions.

What reforms might we implement so as to make the presidency work better? Of course, we want presidents with skill, judgment, experience, flexibility, intelligence, and vision. But even if we had an FDR, he would still face enormous roadblocks. How can we unclog the cholesterol-blocked arteries of the American system?

First, presidents must be *educators* and *visionaries*. Second, presidents must be *coalition builders*, opening lines of communication with Congress and developing bonds of mutual interest. Third, we should eliminate the twenty-second amendment's ban preventing presidents from seeking more than two terms. This might help re-politicize the president's second term and reinvigorate the political leverage of what have become "lame duck" presidents. And finally, we should synchronize the electoral terms of the president and Congress, with all (House, Senate, *and* president) serving four-year terms. This would give the president a greater opportunity to gain an electoral mandate and to govern with a stronger party.

These changes, reforms in the public, the Congress, *and* the presidency, should be seen not in isolation but in relation to one another. They are not a panacea, none exists; but they are designed to revive and reinvigorate the deadlocked separation of powers by fostering greater connection and cooperation. As Woodrow Wilson noted, "The rule of government action is necessary cooperation."[329]

The responsibility for reforming the presidency and the American political system generally falls upon the public, not upon our "leaders." Leaders rarely lead. They rarely can. Usually, leaders are mere officeholders who follow the public's mood or serve as caretakers. Unusual is the officeholder who truly tries to lead, to move the nation, to foment genuine (as opposed to cosmetic) change. We have no one to look to but ourselves. The American citizenry must re-create, empower, and reinvigorate American democracy: government of the people, by the people, and for the people.

But to do this, the American public must wake up and not passively accept the pretty word pictures painted by presidents who are better suited to filling the role of android game show host than to that of governing the nation. Perhaps the low point of the "citizen as ostrich" era came during the early 1980s, when we elected a president who promised the most absurdly farfetched things, and we believed him! Ronald Reagan told us what we wanted to hear; he flattered us to death: huge tax cuts, huge defense increases, no pain, all gain. The president as Pied Piper played a magical tune and we followed, driving a beautiful new car (made in Japan or Germany), paid for on credit, all the way to the poorhouse.

How did this happen? James David Barber reminds us that we would rather live in Oz than Kansas, but even so, where was our Toto, the little dog who pulled back the Wizard's curtain to reveal that the Wizard was no wizard at all but a wrinkly old charlatan? Without a rebirth of citizen politics, new wizards can arise to mislead us. We must not let the pretty promises of photogenic people lead us to suspend our healthy skepticism so necessary in a robust and lively democracy.

If we are going to make the presidency and the American political system "work," we must decide what we want of government and of the presidency: an elective monarch? servant of the people? ruler of the people? a coequal branch of government? The presidency is confused because we are confused.

The failure of leadership in the United States cannot be resolved overnight. The roots of the crisis run deep in our traditions, culture, and structure of government. Reforms such as those previously mentioned might help, but reforms can only do so much and go so far. If we as a people do not know in which direction we wish to go, no leader can do much to take command of the American system.

✪ CONCLUSION

As should be clear, the presidency is a dynamic, not a static institution. While there are standard role expectations and responsibilities faced by all occupants of the office, such uniformity must be seen as the other side of the coin of the rich variety each president brings to the office.

Each president brings a unique set of skills, experiences, goals, and styles to the presidency, but the office itself places certain demands on the president. It is this mix of the unique and the expected that makes the presidency such a fascinating institution. Since all presidents are expected to "lead," how individual differences (both inter- and intrapresidential) impact upon the institution often give us a clue of how well or poorly a president will perform. But being president is often like running in the sand; no matter how much energy you expend, you get nowhere slowly. Presidents rarely get to run on cinder tracks. In the United States, the president may be in office, but he is not necessarily in power.

The problems that plague the presidency (and the American political system) are not entirely new. Past presidents faced many of the anti-leadership obstacles that have confronted the recent occupants of the White House. Many of the problems inhibiting presidential leadership (e.g., intent of the Framers, structure of government) represent historical continuities, not radical departures from the past. All presidents have presided over a system that put leaders in chains. But there *are* some newer elements to add to the leadership aversion system that inhibits presidents (e.g., the decline of party support, weakness of congressional leadership, decline of U.S. power). The leadership aversion system is a constant reality; the components that make up its totality may change over time.

In order to attain progress and not merely change, we must know what to do (vision), how to go about doing it (skill), and hope that the system can be moved in that direction (resources and opportunity).

The United States is a *presidentially driven* system. Without presidential leadership it is nearly impossible for the government to sustain concerted action. While there are times and issues upon which the Congress takes the initiative and leads, this must be seen as the exception rather than the rule.[330]

While the "living" Constitution has evolved to Hamiltonian proportions, the written document still clings to a Madisonian architecture. To modern-day Hamiltonians, the Constitution is an empowering document; to Madisonians, it is a restricting document. In reality, it conforms to Corwin's dictum that it is an "invitation to struggle" for control of power. Since power floats in the American system, someone must grab and hold on to it. But power is slippery. The person best positioned to grab onto power (if only for a limited time) is the president. Thus, presidential leadership is important, perhaps indispensable if the machinery of government is to move ahead.

While power is sometimes abused, often misused, and usually poorly used, we should not forget that the office and powers of the presidency are *potential* powers. And the power to do harm exists with the power to do good. If the presidency of the modern era has not been able to translate power potential into practical good, it must be remembered that it is not power itself that is good or ill, but the uses to which power is put. One could use government power to achieve good ends, but first, one must be able to use the power of government.

In this sense, the United States needs presidential power. The president must be a leader, but not just any kind of leader. Presidents must have the power to do good, but the system of checks and balances is important to put a halt to presidents whose actions may be suspect. Presidents need the power to achieve the ideals grounded in the Declaration of Independence and Bill of Rights, but the citizen needs the separation of powers to control abuse.

Perhaps that is why, as messy, confusing, frustrating, and aggravating as the separation of powers *can be*, it may still offer us the best available model for governing. If made to work properly—presidential leadership and persuasion moving the public around a vision that in turn leads to presidential influence in Congress—the separation of powers, and the theory of government that animates it, offers an opportunity for the government to be both powerful and democratically accountable.[331] In this way, respect for and reinvigoration of the separation of powers may offer presidents a way to overcome the failure so endemic in the American system.

Presidential failure has become a reason (or excuse) for citizen cynicism and despair. The effect of failure and abuse of power on civic participation and participatory democracy has been devastating. Our citizens are democratic dropouts.

Thomas Cronin concluded his "Superman" article by noting that "we pay a price . . . for the way we have over-idealized the presidency." We also pay a price for overdenigrating the presidency. It becomes a self-fulfilling prophesy. We elect a president and almost immediately savage him.

In many ways, the presidency *is* a weak office. Designed with limits and checks, it takes a strong, forceful president in unusual times to overcome the limitations inherent in the office. To transcend weakness, presidents have pursued a combination of the following means: (1) the *formal* power to command; (2) the *informal* power to persuade and bargain; and (3) the *illegal* means of going beyond the law. As presidents get more and more frustrated by their inability to move the machinery of government with the first two methods, they are tempted to resort to the third. Can we have a presidency that is powerful, accountable, *and* constitutional?

The new textbook image of presidential weakness is a recognition of and response to twenty-five years of presidential failure or inadequacy. Can the presidency be saved? In 1980, Thomas Cronin wrote that "the cult of the strong presidency is alive and well. . . . The American public . . . has not lost hope in the efficacy of strong purposive leadership."[332] The goal is to develop a responsive and responsible, powerful but accountable, constitutional and creative presidency. Waiting for Godot, or FDR, will not provide an answer.

The president is not Superman. In a democracy, all citizens are the Clark Kents, waiting to metamorphose into Super men and women. But, by the same token, the U.S. government is (almost always) a presidentially driven system. We need presidential leadership within democratic bounds. We need democratic leadership.

✪ FOR DISCUSSION

1. Write a new Constitution, one that fits the needs of the nation as it enters the twenty-first century.

2. In a post-hegemonic era, can we reduce the power of the president (and the role of the United States in the world) over foreign affairs?

3. Is strong presidential leadership compatible with political democracy? Does a strong presidency make for a weak people?

4. Should the president be a problem solver or an enabler/empowerer for the people?

✪ DEBATE QUESTIONS

I. Resolved: That in the post–Cold War era, the president's power should be reduced in foreign affairs.

II. Resolved: That the United States should switch to a parliamentary form of government, similar to that of Great Britain.

POSTSCRIPT ON THE 1994 MIDTERM ELECTIONS

ACCOMMODATION OR ACRIMONY

As this book goes to press, the Republican party has just captured control of both the Senate and the House of Representatives. The former was expected, the latter comes as something of a surprise. The resentment of the voters came out in the voting booths; the ins were thrown out, and the outs were voted in.

Even relatively popular and successful incumbents such as Governor Ann Richards of Texas, Governor Mario Cuomo of New York, and Tennessee Senator Jim Sasser (all Democrats) were defeated. And while the Democrats did win several big-ticket races (Robb over North in Virginia and Feinstein over Huffington in California), overall, the Democrats got trounced. Why?

Several factors seemed to coalesce: growing voter frustration with government, disapproval of President Clinton (in the 1992 election, candidate Clinton had no presidential coattails; in the 1994 midterm elections, he seemed to be issuing exit visas), the weight of several congressional scandals coming home to roost, and a broader sense that people were afraid for the future—that they were confused and scared not just about where the nation was going, but what impact the fast-paced changes in the world would have on their future. The world was confused and confusing, and people seemed to have no compass to guide them. The focus on anger and confusion turned on the Congress. Incumbents were an endangered species.

Given that the Republicans now control the House, the Senate, and the Supreme Court, most of the key governorships, and many state legislatures, where does that leave Bill Clinton, the lone Democrat in a sea of Republican officeholders?

It is difficult to exert presidential control when conditions are ripe for leadership, but Bill Clinton has now been dealt a terrible political hand. In this atmosphere, leadership becomes incredibly difficult.

How do you devise a governing strategy when your political adversaries control most of the levers of power? If the only way to govern legitimately is to gain cooperation and consensus, is there any way for the president and Congress to work together?

In past years, divided government meant a Republican in the White House and Democratic control in the Congress. Now, the institutional divisions have flip-flopped. What stands in the way of productive cooperation within a divided government?

We should not expect a great deal from the next two years of the Clinton presidency. His power position is very tenuous, and his opposition is well organized, well funded, and smells political blood.

The Republicans will act on the basis of self-interest, just as the Democrats did when they controlled Congress. What is their self-interest? To help Bill Clinton become a successful president? Hardly. What advantage is there for the Republicans if Clinton is seen as a winner?

Self-interest compels the Republicans to make Bill Clinton look bad. If Clinton looks good, he may win the presidency in 1996. And several prominent congressional Republicans (Senator Bob Dole, for example) are already running for president. Why should Dole help Clinton? If he does, it will only diminish his chances in 1996.

In our system of separation of powers, when different parties control the Congress and the White House, institutional conflict, not cooperation, is likely.* Gridlock usually results. Should we expect otherwise?† After all, Bill Clinton is the political adversary of Bob Dole and the Republicans. Why aid their cause? (And don't say "because it is for the good of the nation": given the negative nature of 1994's campaigning, the good of the nation seemed lost amid the harsh accusations). Helping Clinton hurts the Republicans' chances of winning the presidency in 1996. Expect gridlock.

This state of affairs would not be possible in a parliamentary democracy such as Great Britain. There, a fusion of legislative and executive powers exists. If the United States had such a system, Bill Clinton would not have been able to survive the November 8 massacre. The Republicans would have taken control of the White House in a parliamentary system.

But under the separation of powers, divided government once again becomes a political reality. And no one is in charge, no one is responsible, no one is to blame. Bill Clinton will blame an obstructionist Congress for his problems; the Republicans will blame Bill Clinton. They will both be right. But if we wish to point the finger of blame for gridlock we should also look to the system which separates, divides, and shares powers. It should be a bumpy ride.

---

*James L. Sundquist, "Needed: A Political Theory for the New Era of Coalition Government In the United States," Political Science Quarterly 103, winter 1988.
†For a contrary view, see David R. Mayhew, Divided We Govern (New Haven: Yale University Press, 1991).

★★★

ENDNOTES

PREFACE

1. David R. Mayhew, *Congress: The Electoral Connection* (New Haven: Yale University Press, 1974).
2. The power maximizing part of this theory is drawn from the pioneering work of Richard E. Neustadt, whose book *Presidential Power* (New York: Wiley, 1960) is still considered a classic work on presidential politics. The second part of the theory concerning the limits of power is drawn from Thomas E. Cronin's discussion of Neustadt's work that appears in *The State of the Presidency* (Boston: Little, Brown, 1980), pp. 121–136.
3. Michael A. Genovese, ed., *Women as National Leaders* (Newbury Park, Calif.: Sage, 1993).

CHAPTER I

4. Phil Williams, "The Limits of American Power: From Nixon to Reagan," *International Affairs*, autumn 1987.
5. Thomas E. Cronin, *The State of the Presidency* (Boston: Little, Brown, 1980), p. vi.
6. Theodore J. Lowi and Benjamin Ginsberg, *Democrats Return to Power* (New York: Norton, 1994), p. 2.
7. John Chubb and Paul Peterson, eds., *Can the Government Govern?* (Washington, D.C.: Brookings, 1989).
8. Larry Berman, *Lyndon Johnson's War* (New York: Norton, 1991).
9. Michael A. Genovese, *The Nixon Presidency: Power and Politics in Turbulent Times*, (Westport, Conn.: Greenwood, 1990).
10. Roger Porter, "Gerald Ford: A Healing Presidency," in Fred I. Greenstein, ed., *Leadership in the Modern Presidency* (Cambridge: Harvard University Press, 1988), pp. 199–227.
11. Erwin C. Hargrove, *Jimmy Carter as President: A Study of Policy Leadership* (Baton Rouge: Louisiana State University Press, 1988).
12. Lou Cannon, *President Reagan: The Role of a Lifetime* (New York: Touchstone, 1991).
13. Colin Campbell and Bert A. Rockman, *The Bush Presidency: First Appraisals*. (Chatham, N.J.: Chatham House, 1991).
14. William E. Leuchtenburg, *In the Shadow of FDR: From Harry Truman to Ronald Reagan* (Ithaca, N.Y.: Cornell University Press, 1983). See also Philip Abbott, *The Exemplary Presidency* (Amherst: University of Massachusetts Press, 1990).
15. Terry M. Moe, "Presidential Style and Presidential Theory," paper presented at the Presidency Research Conference, Pittsburgh, Pa., 1990, p. 8.
16. Thomas E. Cronin, "Superman, Our Textbook President," *The Washington Monthly*, October 1970.
17. Robert J. Spitzer, *President and Congress* (New York: McGraw-Hill, 1992), pp. 36–37.

18. Fred I. Greenstein, *The Hidden-Hand Presidency: Eisenhower as Leader* (New York: Basic Books, 1982).

19. Adapted from William G. Andrews, "The Presidency, Congress, and Constitutional Theory," in Norman C. Thomas, ed., *The Presidency in Contemporary Context* (New York: Dodd, Mead, 1973). Andrews refers only to two categories of evaluation, "Hallowed Be the President" and "Deliver Us from Presidents." I have added all others.

20. Alfred DeGrazia, *Congress and the Presidency* (Washington, D.C.: American Enterprise Institute, 1967) and *Republic in Crisis: Congress Against the Executive Force* (New York: Federal Legal Publications, 1965).

21. Richard E. Neustadt, *Presidential Power: The Politics of Leadership* (New York: Free Press, 1990).

22. Clinton Rossiter, *The American Presidency* (New York: Harcourt, Brace & World, 1956), p. 250.

23. Ibid., p. 251.

24. Neustadt, *Presidential Power*, p. 195.

25. Thomas E. Cronin, *The State of the Presidency*, 2nd ed. (Boston: Little, Brown, 1980), pp. 75–116. See also William W. Lammers, *Presidential Politics* (New York: HarperCollins, 1976); and Richard M. Pious, *The American Presidency* (New York: Basic Books, 1979).

26. Herman Finer, *The Presidency* (Chicago: University of Chicago Press, 1960), pp. 111 and 119.

27. James MacGregor Burns, *Presidential Government: The Crucible of Leadership* (Boston: Houghton Mifflin, 1965), p. 330.

28. Grant McConnell, *The Modern Presidency* (New York: St. Martin's Press, 1967), p. 87.

29. Albert Cantrill, *The American People, Vietnam, and the Presidency* (Princeton: Princeton University Press, 1976); David Halberstan, *The Best and the Brightest* (New York: Random House, 1972); Stanley Karnow, *Vietnam: A History* (New York: Viking, 1983).

30. Berman, *Lyndon Johnson's War*.

31. Genovese, *The Nixon Presidency*.

32. Michael A. Genovese, "Presidential Corruption: A Framework," paper presented at annual meeting of the American Political Science Association, New York, September 1–5, 1994.

33. Arthur M. Schlesinger, Jr., *The Imperial Presidency* (Boston: Houghton Mifflin, 1973).

34. Marcus Cunliffe, "A Defective Institution?" *Commentary*, February 1968, p. 28.

35. Schlesinger, *The Imperial Presidency*.

36. Quoted in Joseph Kraft, "The Post Imperial Presidency," *New York Times*, November 2, 1980, p. 31.

37. Michael A. Genovese, *The Presidency in an Age of Limits* (Westport, Conn.: Greenwood Press, 1993), chap. 3.

38. For a more extensive analysis of the modern presidents, see Genovese, *The Presidency in an Age of Limits*.

39. Genovese, "Presidential Corruption."

40. See Terrel H. Bell, *The Thirteenth Man: A Reagan Cabinet Memoir* (New York: Free Press, 1987); Alexander M. Haig, Jr., *Caveat: Realism, Reagan and Foreign Policy* (New York: Macmillan, 1984); David A. Stockman, *The Triumph of Politics: The Inside Story of the Reagan Revolution* (New York: Avon, 1987); Michael K. Deaver, *Behind the Scenes* (New York: William Morrow, 1988); Larry Speakes, *Speaking Out* (New York: Scribners, 1988); Donald T. Regan, *For the Record: From Wall Street to Washington* (New York: Harcourt Brace Jovanovich, 1988).

41. Michael A. Genovese, "The Return of the Imperial Presidency," *Presidency Research*, fall 1986.

42. For a full account of how the modern U.S. presidents understood and attempted to deal with the decline of U.S. power, see Genovese, *The Presidency in an Age of Limits*.

43. Michael Nelson, "Evaluating the Presidency," in Nelson, *The Presidency and the Political System* (Washington, D.C.: CQ Press, 1984), p. 10.

44. Cronin, "Superman: Our Textbook President."

45. Michael A. Genovese, "Wimpyman, Our Textbook President," *Presidency Research*, winter 1988–89.

46. George Will, "The Veep and the Blatherskite," *Newsweek*, June 29, 1992, p. 72.

47. Lowi and Ginsberg, *Democrats Return to Power*, p. 18.

48. Harold M. Barger, *The Impossible Presidency: Illusions and Realities of Executive Power* (Glenview, Ill.: Scott, Foresman, 1984), p. 2.

49. Ibid., p. 12.

50. Godfrey Hodgson, *All Things to All Men* (New York: Touchstone, 1980), p. 13.

51. Robert K. Murray and T. H. Blessing, "The Presidential Performance Study: A Progress Report," *Journal of American History* 170 (1983). Reagan is included in a 1991 update of the survey.

52. Stephen Skowronek, "Presidential Leadership in Political Time," in Michael Nelson, ed., *The Presidency and the Political System*, 4th ed. (Washington, D.C.: CQ Press, 1994).

53. Jimmy Breslin, *How The Good Guys Finally Won* (New York: Ballantine, 1975), p. 29.

54. Schlesinger, *The Imperial Presidency*, p. 431. See also Robert E. DiClerico, *The American President* (Englewood Cliffs, N.J.: Prentice-Hall, 1979).

55. James David Barber, "The Nixon Brush with Tyranny," *Political Science Quarterly*, winter 1977–78, p. 581.

56. Peter Drucker, *The Effective Executive* (New York: HarperCollins, 1966), p. 79.

CHAPTER 2

57. Hugh Heclo and Lester Salamon, *The Illusion of Presidential Government* (Boulder, Colo.: Westview Press, 1981), p. 1.

58. Quoted in Thomas E. Cronin, "Presidential Power Revised and Reappraised," *Western Political Quarterly* 32, no. 4 (December 1979), p. 381.

59. Alexander Hamilton, James Madison, and John Jay, *The Federalist Papers*, no. 51 (New York: New American Library, 1961), p. 322.

60. Madison, *Federalist*, no. 45; Hamilton, *Federalist*, no. 70, respectively.

61. Edward S. Corwin, *The President: Office and Powers, 1978–1984*, 5th ed. (New York: New York University Press, 1984), originally published in 1940. See also Joseph M. Bessette and Jeffrey Tulis, *The Presidency in the Constitutional Order* (Baton Rouge: Louisiana State University Press, 1981); and Louis Fisher, *The Constitution Between Friends* (New York: St. Martin's Press, 1978).

62. Thomas E. Cronin, ed., *Inventing the American Presidency* (Lawrence: University Press of Kansas, 1989).

63. Lyn Ragsdale, *Presidential Politics* (Boston: Houghton Mifflin, 1993), p. 30.

64. Bert A. Rockman, *The Leadership Question: The Presidency and the American System* (New York: Praeger, 1984), p. 42.

65. James P. Pfiffner, *The Modern Presidency* (New York: St. Martin's Press, 1993), p. 13.

66. Rockman, *The Leadership Question*, pp. 39, 40, 41.

67. David Mayhew argues in *Divided We Govern* (New Haven: Yale University Press, 1991) that divided government *has not* had a significant impact upon deadlock/gridlock. For works that see divided government as a problem, see Lance T. LeLoup and Steven A. Shull, *Congress and the President: The Policy Connection* (Belmont, Calif.: Wadsworth, 1993); James A. Thurber, *Divided Democracy* (Washington, D.C.: CQ Press, 1991); and Gary W. Cox and Samuel Kernell, *The Politics of Divided Government* (Boulder, Colo.: Westview Press, 1991). For an excellent overview, see Charles O. Jones, *The Presidency in a Separated System* (Washington, D.C.: Brookings, 1994); and Donald L. Robinson, *"To the Best of My Ability": The Presidency and the Constitution* (New York: Norton, 1987).

68. Rockman, *The Leadership Question*, p. 43.

69. Arthur M. Schlesinger, Jr., "Leave the Constitution Alone," in Donald Robinson, ed., *Reforming American Government: The Bicentennial Papers of the Committee on the Constitutional System* (Boulder, Colo.: Westview Press, 1985), p. 53.

70. Neustadt, *Presidential Power*.

71. James MacGregor Burns, "More Than Merely Power: II," *New York Times*, November 17, 1978, p. A29.

72. For an excellent overview of Gardner's views on leadership, see John Gardner, *On Leadership* (New York: Free Press, 1990).

73. Clinton Rossiter, *Conservatism in America* (New York: Vintage, 1962), p. 72.

74. Cronin, *The State of the Presidency*, p. 24.

75. Max Lerner, *America as a Civilization* (New York: Knopf, 1957), p. 718.

76. Alexis de Tocqueville, *Democracy in America* (New York: Knopf, 1969), p. 430.

77. Michel Crozier, *The Trouble with America* (Berkeley: University of California Press, 1984), p. 71.

78. See Robert Bellah, Richard Masden, William Sullivan, Ann Swidel, and Steven Tipton, *Habits of the Heart* (New York: HarperCollins, 1985).

79. Warren Bennis, *Why Leaders Can't Lead: The Unconscious Conspiracy Continues* (San Francisco: Jossey-Bass, 1989), p. 46.

80. David F. Schuman, *A Preface of Politics* (Itasca, Ill.: F. E. Peacock, 1991), p. 6.

81. Samuel P. Huntington, *American Politics: The Promise of Disharmony* (Cambridge: Harvard University Press, 1981), pp. 4, 33.

82. Madison, *Federalist*, no. 10.

83. See Stephen Skowronek, *The Politics Presidents Make* (Cambridge, Mass.: Belknap Press, 1993).

84. Rockman, *The Leadership Question*, p. 84.

85. Stephen Skowronek, "Presidential Leadership in Political Time," in Michael J. Nelson, ed., *The President and the Political System*, 3rd ed. (Washington, D.C.: CQ Press, 1990), pp. 117–162.

86. See Michael A. Genovese, "Presidential Leadership and Crisis Management," *Presidential Studies Quarterly*, spring 1986, pp. 300–309.

87. Valerie Bunce, *Do New Leaders Make a Difference?: Executive Succession and Public Policy Capitalism and Socialism* (Princeton: Princeton University Press, 1981).

88. Paul C. Light, *The President's Agenda* (Baltimore: Johns Hopkins University Press, 1982).

89. Arthur M. Schlesinger, Jr., *The Cycles of American History* (Boston: Houghton Mifflin, 1986), pp. 22–27.

90. Ibid. p. 34.

91. Erwin C. Hargrove, *The Power of the Modern Presidency* (New York: Knopf, 1974), p. 186.

92. Ibid.

93. Ibid., p. 187.

94. Thomas E. Cronin, "If Bush Is to Be the 'Education President' Much Work Must Be Done at the Grassroots," *Chronicle of Higher Education* 35 (February 1, 1989), pp. B, 2.

95. Ibid, p. 2.

96. James MacGregor Burns, *Leadership* (New York: HarperCollins, 1978).

97. James W. Davis, *The President as Party Leader* (New York: Praeger, 1992). See also Sidney M. Milkis, *The President and the Parties* (New York: Oxford University Press, 1993).

98. James MacGregor Burns, *The Power to Lead: The Crisis of the American Presidency* (New York: Simon & Schuster, 1984), p. 214.

99. Quoted in Richard Hofstadter, *The Idea of a Party System* (Oxford: Oxford University Press, 1969), p. 123.

100. George C. Edwards, *At the Margins: Presidential Leadership in Congress* (New Haven: Yale University Press, 1989).

101. Samuel M. Kernell, *Going Public: New Strategies of Presidential Leadership* (Washington D.C.: Congressional Quarterly Press, 1986).

102. Milkis, *The President and the Parties*, p. 10; and Craig A. Rimmerman, *Presidency by Plebiscite* (Boulder, Colo.: Westview Press, 1993).

103. Lester G. Seligman and Cary R. Covington, *The Coalitional Presidency* (Chicago: Dorsey Press, 1989).

104. Burns, *The Power to Lead*, p. 43.

105. See Richard A. Watson, *The Presidential Contest* (New York: Wiley, 1984); Stephen J. Wayne, *The Road to the White House* (New York: St. Martin's Press, 1988); Nelson W. Polsby and Aaron Wildavsky, *Presidential Elections* (New York, Free Press, 1991); Herbert B. Asher, *Presidential Elections and American Politics* (Homewood, Ill.: Dorsey Press, 1984); and James W. Ceasar, *Presidential Selection* (Princeton: Princeton University Press, 1979).

106. James A. Barnes, "Ready or Not," *National Journal*, September 4, 1993, pp. 2136–2141.

107. Hubert Humphrey, quoted in the *New York Times*, October 13, 1974, p. E18. Quoted in: Herbert B. Asher, *Presidential Elections and American Politics* (Homewood, Ill.: Dorsey Press, 1984), p. 186. See also Anthony Corrado, *Creative Campaigning* (Boulder, Colo.: Westview Press, 1992); John H. Kessel, *Presidential Campaign Politics* (Chicago: Dorsey Press, 1988); and Joseph A. Pika, Zelna Mosley, and Richard A. Watson, *The Presidential Contest* (Washington, D.C.: Congressional Quarterly Press, 1992).

108. Charles E. Lindblom, "The Market as Prison," *The Journal of Politics* 44 (1982): 324–336.

109. Ibid., p. 325.

110. Ibid.

111. Ibid., pp. 328–329.

112. James O'Connor, *The Fiscal Crisis of the State* (New York: St. Martin's Press, 1973); and Alan Wolfe, *The Limits of Legitimacy* (New York: Free Press, 1977).

113. Edward S. Greenberg, *The American Political System* (Boston: Little, Brown, 1986), p. 344. See also William F. Grover, *The President as Prisoner* (New York: SUNY Press, 1989).

114. See Ray C. Fair, "The Effect of Economic Events on Votes for President," *Review of Economics and Statistics* 60 (1978): 159–173; David G. Golden and James M. Poterba, "The Price of Popularity: The Political Business Cycle Reexamined," *American Journal of Political Science* 24 (1980): 696–714; and Sam Kernell, "Explaining Presidential Popularity," *American Political Science Review* 72 (1978): 506–522.

115. See Frank E. Meyers, "Social Classes and Political Change in Western Industrial Systems," *Comparative Politics* 2 (1970): 389–412.
116. Quoted in Arthur M. Schlesinger, Jr., *A Thousand Days: John F. Kennedy in the White House* (Boston: Houghton Mifflin, 1965), p. 641.
117. Quoted in Ronald F. King, "The Politics of Regressive Taxation Changes," paper prepared for delivery at the 1977 annual meeting of the Midwest Political Science Association, p. 12.
118. Thomas E. Cronin, "Presidential Power Revised and Reappraised," *Western Political Quarterly* 32 (1979): 389.
119. Bruce Miroff, *Pragmatic Illusions* (New York: David McKay, 1976), p. 273.
120. Ibid., p. 274.
121. Ibid., p. 276.
122. Harold Kongju Koh, *The National Security Constitution: Sharing Power After the Iran-Contra Affair* (New Haven: Yale University Press, 1990).
123. For two opposing views of U.S. decline, see Paul Kennedy, *The Rise and Fall of the Great Powers* (New York: Vintage, 1987); and Joseph Nye, *Bound to Lead* (New York: Basic Books, 1990).
124. Genovese, *The Presidency in an Age of Limits*.
125. Richard Rose, *The Postmodern President: George Bush Meets the World* (Chatham, N.J.: Chatham House, 1991), p. 25.
126. Ibid., p. 3.
127. Ibid.
128. Ibid., pp. 27–28.
129. Ibid., p. 4.

CHAPTER 3

130. Hedrick Smith, *The Power Game: How Washington Works* (New York: Ballantine, 1988).
131. Michael A. Genovese and Seth Thompson, "Women as Chief Executives: Does Gender Matter?" in Michael A. Genovese, ed., *Women as National Leaders*, (Newbury Park, Calif.: Sage, 1993), pp. 1–2.
132. Cronin, *The State of the Presidency*, p. 145.
133. Robert Shogan, *The Riddle of Power* (New York: Dutton, 1991), p. 5.
134. Robert A. Dahl, *Pluralist Democracy in the United States* (New York: Rand McNally, 1967), p. 90.
135. James P. Pfiffner, *The Strategic Presidency: Hitting the Ground Running* (Chicago: Dorsey Press, 1988).
136. James MacGregor Burns, *Roosevelt: The Lion and the Fox* (San Diego: Harvest/HBJ, 1984), p. 197.
137. Edward S. Corwin, *The President: Office and Powers* (New York: New York University Press, 1957).
138. E. Neustadt, *Presidential Power*.
139. Burns, *Leadership*, p. 18.
140. John F. Kennedy, Foreword to Theodore C. Sorenson, *Decision-Making in the White House* (New York: Columbia University Press, 1963), p. xi.
141. Burns, *Leadership*, part 3.
142. Donald T. Phillips, *Lincoln on Leadership* (New York: Warner, 1992), p. 137.
143. Burt Nanus, *Visionary Leadership* (San Francisco: Jossey-Bass, 1992), p. 3.
144. Ibid., p. 4.

145. Sheldon Wolin, *Politics and Vision* (Boston: Little, Brown, 1960), p. 436.

146. Warren Bennis and Burt Nanus, *Leaders: Strategies for Taking Charge* (New York: HarperCollins, 1985), pp. 39, 42.

147. Lester Salamon, *The Illusion of Presidential Government* (Boulder, Colo.: Westview Press, 1981), p. 292.

148. Lance Blakesley, *The President as a Strategically Versatile Leader* (Chicago: Nelson-Hall, forthcoming, 1995).

149. Quoted in Sidney Blumenthal, "The Education of a President," *The New Yorker*, January 24, 1994, p. 33.

150. Fred I. Greenstein and Nelson Polsby, eds., *The Handbook of Political Theory: Micro-Political Theory* (Reading, Pa.: Addison-Wesley, 1975), pp. 19–21.

151. Erwin C. Hargrove, "Presidential Personality and Leadership Style," in George C. Edwards III, John H. Kessel, and Bert A. Rockman, eds., *Researching the Presidency: Vital Questions, New Approaches* (Pittsburgh: University of Pittsburgh Press, 1993), p. 70.

152. Ibid., p. 82.

153. Ibid., p. 69.

154. For a view which suggests we should spend less time studying skill and more on institutional pressures, see Terry M. Moe, "Presidents, Institutions, and Theory," in Edwards, Kessel, and Rockman, op. cit., pp. 337–385.

155. Robert K. Murray and Tim H. Blessing, *Greatness in the White House: Rating the Presidents, Washington Through Carter* (University Park: Pennsylvania State University Press, 1988).

156. Burns, *Roosevelt: The Lion and the Fox*, p. 264.

157. See James David Barber's oft criticized but influential work, *The Presidential Character: Predicting Performance in the White House* (Englewood Cliffs, N.J.: Prentice Hall, 1992).

158. James P. Pfiffner, ed., *The Managerial Presidency* (Pacific Grove, Calif.: Brooks/Cole, 1991).

159. Pfiffner, *The Strategic Presidency*.

160. For an excellent review of how the press treated President Clinton in the early stages of his administration, see the three-part series by David Shaw, *Los Angeles Times*, September 15, 16, 17, 1993.

161. Pfiffner, *The Strategic Presidency*, p. 4.

162. Quoted in Hedrick Smith, *The Power Game*, p. 331.

163. Light, *The President's Agenda*, pp. 41–45.

164. Alexander Haig, *Caveat: Realism, Reagan, and Foreign Policy* (New York: Macmillan, 1984).

165. James P. Pfiffner, "The Carter-Reagan Transition: Hitting the Ground Running," *Presidential Studies Quarterly*, fall 1983.

166. Bunce, *Do New Leaders Make a Difference?*

167. Light, *The President's Agenda*, p. 36.

168. Quoted in Light, *The President's Agenda*, pp. 45–46.

169. See Hedrick Smith, *The Power Game*, pp. 340–342.

170. Thomas P. O'Neill with William Novak, *Man of the House: The Life and Political Memoirs of Speaker Tip O'Neill* (New York: Random House, 1987), p. 273.

171. Seligman and Covington, *The Coalitional Presidency*.

172. Cronin, *The State of the Presidency*, p. 168.

173. Benjamin Ginsberg and Martin Shefter, *Politics by Other Means* (New York: Basic Books, 1990), pp. 164–165.

174. James MacGregor Burns, quoted in Hedrick Smith, *The Power Game*, p. 679.

175. Hedrick Smith, *The Power Game*, p. 680.

176. Ibid.
177. James A. Davis and David L. Nixon, "The President's Party," *Presidential Studies Quarterly* 24:2 (spring 1994): 363–365.
178. Paul Brace and Barbara Hinckley, *Follow the Leader: Opinion Polls and the Modern Presidents* (New York: Basic Books, 1992).
179. Richard E. Neustadt, *Presidential Power and the Modern Presidents* (New York: Free Press, 1990).
180. George C. Edwards, *Presidential Influence in Congress* (San Francisco: Freeman, 1980), pp. 86–100.
181. Neustadt, *Presidential Power*, p. 76.
182. Quoted in George C. Edwards III and Stephen J. Wayne, *Presidential Leadership: Politics and Policy Making* (New York: St. Martin's Press, 1990), p. 90.
183. Edwards and Wayne, op. cit., p. 90.
184. Quoted in Edwards and Wayne, op. cit., p. 91.
185. Jody Powell, quoted in Michael Baruch Grossman and Martha Joynt Kumar, "Carter, Reagan, and the Media: Have the Rules Changed or the Poles of the Spectrum of Success?" (paper presented at the annual meeting of the American Political Science Association, New York, September 3–6, 1981), p. 18.
186. Fred Greenstein, "What the President Means to Americans," in James David Barber, ed., *Choosing the President* (New York: American Assembly, 1974), pp. 130–131.
187. Theodore J. Lowi, *The Personal President: Power Invested Promise Unfulfilled* (Ithaca, N.Y.: Cornell University, 1985).
188. Brace and Hinckley, *Follow the Leader*, p. 1.
189. Jeffrey K. Tulis, *The Rhetorical Presidency* (Princeton: Princeton University Press, 1987), chap. 2, "The Old Way: Founding and Forms."
190. Pfiffner, *The Modern Presidency*, chap. 2.
191. Mary E. Stuckey, *The President as Interpreter-in-Chief* (Chatham, N.J.: Chatham House, 1991).
192. Bruce Miroff, *Icons of Democracy* (New York: Basic Books, 1993), p. 2.
193. Thomas E. Cronin, "Leadership and Democracy," *Liberal Education* 73:2 (March/April 1987): 35–38; and Benjamin R. Barber, "Neither Leaders nor Followers: Citizenship Under Strong Democracy," in Michael R. Beschloss and Thomas E. Cronin, *Essays in Honor of James MacGregor Burns* (Englewood Cliffs, N.J.: Prentice-Hall, 1989), pp. 117–132.
194. Genovese, *The Presidency in an Age of Limits*.
195. Harvey G. Zeidenstein, "Presidents' Popularity and Their Wins and Losses on Major Issues: Does One Have a Greater Influence over the Other?" *Presidential Studies Quarterly*, spring 1985, pp. 287–300.
196. Richard A. Brody, *Assessing the President: The Media, Elite Opinion, and Public Support* (Stanford, Calif.: Stanford University Press, 1991).
197. Ibid.
198. Summaries of the literature on the impact of the economy can be found in Samuel Kernell, *Going Public* (Washington, D.C.: Congressional Quarterly Press, 1986), chap. 7; and George C. Edwards III, *The Public Presidency* (New York: St. Martin's Press, 1983), chap. 6.
199. Robert H. Ferrell, ed., *Off the Record: The Private Papers of Harry S Truman* (New York: HarperCollins, 1980), p. 310.
200. Brace and Hinckley, *Follow the Leader*, p. 45.
201. Roderick Hart, *The Sound of Leadership* (Chicago: University of Chicago Press, 1987).
202. Edwards and Wayne, *Presidential Leadership*, p. 131.
203. Barger, *The Impossible Presidency*, p. 357.

204. John Orman, "Covering the American Presidency: Valanced Reporting in the Presidential Press," *Presidential Studies Quarterly* 14 (1984): 381–382.

205. Norman Ornstein and Michael Robinson, "The Case of Our Disappearing Congress," TV *Guide*, January 11, 1986, pp. 4–10.

206. Hedrick Smith, *The Power Game*, p. 10.

207. Cronin, *The State of the Presidency*, pp. 140–151.

208. Deaver, *Behind the Scenes*, p. 73.

209. John Maltese, *Spin Control: The White House Office of Communications and the Management of Presidential News* (Chapel Hill: University of North Carolina Press, 1992).

210. Hedrick Smith, *The Power Game*, p. 407.

211. Samuel Kernell, *Going Public: New Strategies of Presidential Leadership* (Washington, D.C.: Congressional Quarterly, 1986).

212. Jeffrey K. Tulis, *The Rhetorical Presidency* (Princeton: Princeton University Press, 1987), p. 95.

213. James W. Davis, *The American Presidency: A New Perspective* (New York: HarperCollins, 1987), p. 121.

214. Genovese, *The Nixon Presidency*, chap. 2.

215. Quoted in Michael J. Robinson and Margaret A. Sheehan, *Over the Wire and on TV* (New York: Russell Sage Foundation, 1983), p. 103.

216. Mark Hertsgaard, *On Bended Knee: The Press and the Reagan Presidency* (New York: Schocken Books, 1988).

217. See series by David Shaw, *Los Angeles Times*, September 15, 16, and 17, 1993, for an examination of the media's treatment of the Clinton presidency.

218. Larry Sabato, *Feeding Frenzy* (New York: Free Press, 1991).

219. James S. Young, *The Washington Community, 1800–1828* (New York: Columbia University Press, 1966), pp. 75–76.

220. Emmet John Hughes, *The Living Presidency* (New York: Coward, McCann and Geoghegan, 1973), p. 208.

221. Robert J. Spitzer, *The Presidential Veto: Touchstone of the American Presidency* (Albany: State University of New York Press, 1988).

222. Arthur M. Schlesinger, Jr., and Alfred de Grazia, *Congress and the Presidency. Their Role in Modern Times* (Washington, D.C.: American Enterprise Institute, 1967), pp. 4–5.

223. Robert J. Spitzer, *President and Congress: Executive Hegemony at the Crossroads of American Government* (New York: McGraw-Hill, 1993), p. xx.

224. Lance T. LeLoup and Steven A. Shull, *Congress and the President: The Policy Connection* (Belmont, Calif.: Wadsworth, 1993).

225. Rossiter, *The American Presidency*, p. 26.

226. Roger H. Davidson, "The Presidency and Congress," in Michael Nelson, ed., *The Presidency and the Political System* (Washington, D.C., Congressional Quarterly, 1984), pp. 363–391.

227. George C. Edwards III, *At the Margins: Presidential Leadership in Congress* (New Haven: Yale University Press, 1989).

228. *Youngstown Sheet and Tube Co. v. Sawyer*, 343 US 579,635 (1952).

229. Edwards, *At the Margins*; Jon R. Bond and Richard Fleisher, *The President in the Legislative Arena* (Chicago: University of Chicago Press, 1990).

230. Brace and Hinckley, *Follow the Leader*; see also Douglas Rivers and Nancy Rose, "Passing the President's Program: Public Opinion and Presidential Influence in Congress," *American Journal of Political Science* 29 (May 1985): 183–196; and Richard Brody, *Assessing the President: The Media, Elite Opinion, and Public Support* (Stanford, Calif.: Stanford University Press, 1991), p. 21.

231. Brody, *Assessing the President*, p. 22.

232. Bond and Fleisher, *The President in the Legislative Arena*, p. 218; Edwards, *At the Margins*; and Aage R. Clausen, *How Congressmen Decide: A Policy Focus* (New York: St. Martin's Press, 1973).

233. Terry Sullivan, "Headcounts, Expectations, and Presidential Coalitions in Congress," *American Journal of Political Science* 32:3 (August 1988): 567–589.

234. Edwards, *At the Margins*, p. 216.

235. Quoted in Barger, *The Impossible Presidency*, p. 127.

236. Rowland Evans and Robert Novak, *Lyndon B. Johnson: The Exercise of Power* (New York: New American Library, 1966), p. 104.

237. Quoted in George C. Edwards III, "Legislative Leadership," in Leonard W. Levy and Louis Fisher, eds., *Encyclopedia of the American Presidency* (New York: Simon & Schuster, 1993), vol. 3, p. 950.

238. Douglas Jehl, "Clinton Assails G.O.P. Delays in Bitter Tones," *New York Times*, July 27, 1993, p. A1.

239. See Paul Richter and Karen Tamulty, "Clinton's Use of the Soft Sell Worries Allies," *Los Angeles Times*, July 31, 1993, p. 1.; and R. W. Apple, Jr., "An Excess of the Pulpit and Not Enough Bully," *New York Times*, August 5, 1993, p. A12.

240. James Gerstenzang and Paul Richter, "Clinton Lobbying Wins More Votes for NAFTA Pact," *Los Angeles Times*, November 17, 1993, p. A1.

241. Karen Tamulty, "Clinton Piles Up Record Legislative Wins," *Los Angeles Times*, November 13, 1993, p. A23.

242. Bruce Buchanan, *The Presidential Experience: What the Office Does to the Man* (Englewood Cliffs, N.J.: Prentice-Hall, 1978).

243. For excellent works on the managerial aspects of the presidency, see Pfiffner, *The Managerial Presidency*; Peri E. Arnold, *Making the Managerial Presidency* (Princeton: Princeton University Press, 1986); Colin Campbell, *Managing the Presidency: Carter, Reagan, and the Search for Executive Harmony* (Pittsburgh: University of Pittsburgh Press, 1986); Stephen Hess, *Organizing the Presidency* (Washington, D.C.: Brookings, 1976); Hugh Heclo, *A Government of Strangers: Executive Politics in Washington* (Brookings, 1977); Samuel Kernell and Samuel Popkin, eds., *Chief of Staff* (Berkeley: University of California Press, 1986); and John P. Burke, *The Institutional Presidency* (Baltimore: Johns Hopkins University Press, 1992).

244. Colin Campbell, "Political Executives and Their Officials," in Ada W. Finifter, ed., *Political Science: The State of the Discipline*, II (Washington, D.C.: American Political Science Association, 1993).

245. Bennis and Nanus, *Leaders: The Strategies for Taking Charge*, p. 21.

246. Warren Bennis, *On Becoming a Leader* (Reading, Pa.: Addison-Wesley, 1989), p. 45.

247. James P. Pfiffner, "The President's Chief of Staff: Lessons Learned," Working Paper 92:19, October 1992, The Institute of Public Policy, George Mason University.

248. Richard T. Johnson, *Managing the White House* (New York: HarperCollins, 1974).

249. Richard Nathan, *The Administrative Presidency* (New York: Wiley, 1983).

250. Terry M. Moe, "The Politicized Presidency," in John E. Chubb and Paul E. Peterson, eds., *The New Direction in American Politics* (Washington, D.C.: Brookings, 1985).

251. Aaron Wildavsky, "The Two Presidencies," in *Trans-Action*, December 1966, p. 7. See also Barbara Kellerman and Ryan J. Barilleaux, *The President as World Leader* (New York: St. Martin's Press, 1991); and Cecil V. Crabb and Kevin V. Mulcahy, *American National Security* (Pacific Grove, Calif.: Brooks-Cole, 1991).

252. Lance T. LeLoup and Steven A. Shull, "Congress Versus the Executive: The 'Two Presidencies' Reconsidered," *Social Science Quarterly* 59 (March 1979): 704–719; Lee Sigelman, "A Reassessment of the 'Two Presidencies' Thesis," *Journal of Politics* 41

(November 1979): 1195–1205; exchange between Shull/LeLoup and Sigelman in *Journal of Politics* 43 (May 1981); Jeffrey E. Cohen, "A Historical Reassessment of Wildavsky's 'Two Presidencies' Thesis," *Social Science Quarterly* 63 (September 1982): 549–555. See also Steven A. Shull, ed., *The Two Presidencies: A Quarter Century Assessment* (Chicago: Nelson-Hall, 1991).

253. Duane M. Oldfield and Aaron Wildavsky, "Reconsidering the Two Presidencies," *Society* (July/August 1989), p. 55.

254. James M. Lindsay and Wayne P. Steger, "The 'Two Presidencies' in Future Research: Moving Beyond Roll-Call Analysis," *Congress and the Presidency* 20:2 (Autumn 1993).

255. Bond and Fleisher, *The President in the Legislative Arena*, p. 171.

256. Genovese, "Presidential Leadership and Crisis Management."

257. Marcia Lynn Whicker, James P. Pfiffner, and Raymond A. Moore, eds., *The Presidency and the Persian Gulf War* (Westport, Conn.: Praeger, 1993).

258. R. W. Apple, Jr., "Reagan Curse on Clinton," *New York Times*, August 1, 1993, p. A1; and Sidney Blumenthal, "The Sorcerer's Apprentices," *The New Yorker*, July 9, 1993, p. 29.

259. Michael A. Genovese, "The Supreme Court as a Check on Presidential Power," *Presidential Studies Quarterly*, winter-spring 1976; and Genovese, *The Supreme Court, the Constitution, and Presidential Power* (Landham, Md.: University Press of America, 1980).

260. Glendon Schubert, *The Presidency in the Courts* (Minneapolis: University of Minnesota Press, 1957), p. 4.

261. Ibid., p. 3.

262. Rossiter, *The American Presidency*, pp. 45 and 42.

263. Koh, *The National Security Constitution*; Thomas M. Franck, *Political Questions/Judicial Answers* (Princeton: Princeton University Press, 1992); and Henry J. Abraham, *Justices & Presidents* (New York: Oxford University Press, 1985).

264. David Gray Adler, "The Court and the Ghost of Curtiss-Wright," paper presented at annual meeting of the American Political Science Association, 1989.

265. Genovese, *The Nixon Presidency*; and Stanley K. Kutler, *The Wars of Watergate* (New York: Knopf, 1990).

266. Theodore Diaper, *A Very Thin Line: The Iran-Contra Affairs* (New York: Touchstone, 1991); and Jane Mayer and Doyle McManus, *Landslide: The Unmaking of the President, 1984–1988* (Boston: Houghton Mifflin, 1988).

267. Nancy V. Baker, *Conflicting Loyalties: Law and Politics in the Attorney General's Office, 1789–1990* (Lawrence: University Press of Kansas, 1992); Katy J. Harriger, *Independent Justice: The Federal Special Prosecutor in American Politics* (Lawrence: University Press of Kansas, 1992); and Rebecca Mae Salokar, *The Solicitor General: The Politics of Law* (Philadelphia: Temple University Press, 1992).

268. Terry Eastland, *Energy in the Executive: The Case for the Strong Presidency* (New York: Free Press, 1992); L. Gordon Corvitz and Jeremy A. Rabkin, eds., *The Fettered Presidency: Legal Constraints on the Executive Branch* (Washington, D.C.: American Enterprise Institute, 1989); and Harvey C. Mansfield, Jr., *Taming the Prince: The Ambivalence of Modern Executive Power* (New York: Free Press, 1989).

269. Koh, *The National Security Constitution*.

270. Daniel P. Franklin, *Extraordinary Measures: The Exercise of Prerogative Powers in the United States* (Pittsburgh: University of Pittsburgh Press, 1991).

271. Genovese, "Presidential Leadership and Crisis Management"; and Genovese, "Presidents and Crisis: Developing a Crisis Management System in the Executive Branch," *International Journal on World Peace*, spring 1987.

272. Michael A. Genovese, "Democratic Theory and the Emergency Powers of the President," *Presidential Studies Quarterly*, summer 1979.

273. John Locke, *Treatise on Civil Government and a Letter Concerning Toleration* (New York: Appleton-Century-Crofts, 1937), chap. 14, p. 109.

274. Ibid., p. 113.

275. Jean Jacques Rousseau, *The Social Contract and Discourses* (New York: Dutton, 1950), book 4, chap. 6, p. 123.

276. John Stuart Mill, *Considerations on Representative Government* (New York: Liberal Arts Press, 1958), p. 274.

277. J. Malcolm Smith and Cornelius P. Cotter, *Powers of the President During Crises* (Washington, D.C.: Public Affairs Press, 1960), p. 7.

278. Niccolò Machiavelli, *The Prince and the Discourses* (New York: Modern Library, 1950), book 1, chap. 34, p. 203.

279. Clinton Rossiter, *Constitutional Dictatorship: Crisis Government in the Modern Democracy* (Princeton: Princeton University Press, 1948).

280. Abe Fortas, "The Constitution and the Presidency," *Washington Law Review* 49 (August 1974): 100.

281. Edward S. Corwin, *Total War and the Constitution* (Westminster, Md.: Knopf, 1947), p. 80.

282. Rossiter, *Constitutional Dictatorship*, p. 12.

283. *New York Times*, September 8, 1942, p. 1.

284. Richard M. Pious, *The American Presidency* (New York: Basic Books, 1979), p. 84.

285. Richard Longaker, Introduction to Rossiter, *The Supreme Court and the Commander in Chief*, expanded ed. (Ithaca, N.Y.: Cornell University Press, 1976), p. xii.

286. Genovese, *The Supreme Court, the Constitution, and Presidential Power*, chap. 3.

CHAPTER 4

287. Barger, *The Impossible Presidency*, pp. 396–397.

288. Miroff, *Icons of Democracy*, p. 1.

289. Burns, *Leadership*, p. 9.

290. Glen A. Phelps, *George Washington and American Constitutionalism* (Lawrence, University Press of Kansas, 1993).

291. Quoted in Larry Berman, *The New American Presidency* (Boston: Little, Brown, 1987), p. 339.

292. Genovese, *The Presidency in an Age of Limits*.

293. Koh, *The National Security Constitution*, chap. 9.

294. Norman C. Thomas, Joseph A. Pika, and Richard A. Watson, *The Politics of the Presidency* (Washington, D.C.: CQ Press, 1993), p. 434.

295. Cronin, "Leadership and Democracy," p. 36.

296. Ibid., pp. 36–37.

297. Quoted in Benjamin R. Barber, "Neither Leaders nor Followers," op. cit., p. 117.

298. Quoted in Mark E. Kann, "Challenging Lockean Liberalism in America: The Case of Debs and Hillquit," *Political Theory*, no. 8 (May 1980), p. 214.

299. Adapted from Michael A. Genovese, "Thomas Jefferson and the Vision of Democratic Leadership," *The Journal of Leadership Studies*, June 1994.

300. Cronin, "Leadership and Democracy," p. 36.

301. James Bryce, *The American Commonwealth* (New York: MacMillan, 1888), vol. 2, p. 460.

302. Miroff, *Icons of Democracy*, p. 1.

303. Schlesinger, *The Cycles of American History*, p. 430.
304. Abraham Lincoln, *The Gettysburg Address*. See Mario Cuomo and Harold Holzer, eds., *Lincoln on Democracy* (New York: HarperCollins, 1990).
305. Willard Sterne Randall, *Thomas Jefferson: A Life* (New York: Henry Holt, 1993). See also Merrill D. Peterson, ed., *The Portable Thomas Jefferson* (New York: Viking, 1975).
306. Miroff, *Icons of Democracy*, p. 354.
307. Edwards, Kessel, and Rockman, eds., *Researching the Presidency*.
308. Benjamin R. Barber, *Strong Democracy: Participatory Politics for a New Age* (Berkeley: University of California Press, 1984).
309. Benjamin R. Barber, "Neither Leaders nor Followers," op. cit., p. 117.
310. Theodore C. Sorensen, *Watchmen in the Night* (Cambridge: MIT Press, 1975).
311. Madison, *Federalist*, no. 51.
312. Genovese, "Presidential Corruption."
313. Milkis, *The President and the Parties*.
314. I first heard Thomas Cronin use this phrase; he claims its genesis can be traced to James M. Burns.
315. Quoted in Thomas E. Cronin, "Thinking and Learning About Leadership," *Presidential Studies Quarterly*, winter 1984, p. 31.
316. Miroff, *Icons of Democracy*, chap. 1.
317. Burns, *Roosevelt: The Lion and the Fox*, p. 151.
318. James L. Sundquist, *Constitutional Reform and Effective Government* (Washington, D.C.: Brookings, 1986); James MacGregor Burns, *The Power to Lead: The Crisis of the American Presidency* (New York: Simon & Schuster, 1984); Donald L. Robinson *"To the Best of My Ability."*
319. For an examination of how Margaret Thatcher used the power of her office to achieve policy and political goals, see Michael A. Genovese, "Margaret Thatcher and the Politics of Conviction Leadership," in Genovese, ed., *Women as National Leaders*, pp. 177–210.
320. Lloyd Cutler, "Party Government Under the Constitution," in Donald L. Robinson, ed., *Reforming American Government: The Bicentennial Papers of the Committee on the Constitutional System* (Boulder, Colo.: Westview Press, 1985); and Sundquist, *Constitutional Reform and Effective Government*.
321. See Terry Eastland, *Energy in the Executive: The Case for the Strong Presidency* (New York: Free Press, 1992); L. Gordon Corvitz and Jeremy A. Rabkin, *The Fettered Presidency: Legal Constraints on the Executive Branch* (Washington, D.C.: American Enterprise Institute, 1989); and Harvey C. Mansfield, Jr., *Taming the Prince: The Ambivalence of Modern Executive Power* (New York: Free Press, 1989).
322. See Cronin, *The State of the Presidency*; Koh, *The National Security Constitution*; and Spitzer, *President and Congress*.
323. Rockman, *The Leadership Question*, p. 221.
324. Quoted in Berman, *The New American Presidency*, p. 344.
325. See LeLoup and Shull, *Congress and the President*.
326. See: Spitzer, *President and Congress*, and Koh, *The National Security Constitution*.
327. Robert Jay Lifton, *The Protean Self: Resilience in an Age of Fragmentation* (New York: Basic Books, 1993).
328. David Osborne and Ted Gaebler, *Reinventing Government* (New York: Plume, 1992).
329. Woodrow Wilson, *The State* (Boston: D. C. Heath, 1903), p. 639.
330. LeLoup and Shull, *Congress and the President*.
331. Spitzer, *President and Congress*.
332. Cronin, *The State of the Presidency*.

★★

BIBLIOGRAPHY

Abbott, Philip. *The Exemplary Presidency*. Amherst: University of Massachusetts Press, 1990.

Abraham, Henry J. *Justices and Presidents*. New York: Oxford University Press, 1985.

Adler, David G. "The Court and the Ghost of Curtiss-Wright." Paper presented at the annual meeting of the American Political Science Association, Washington, D.C., September 1989.

Andrews, William G. "The Presidency, Congress and Constitutional Theory." In *The Presidency in Contemporary Context*, edited by Norman C. Thomas. New York: Dodd, Mead, 1973.

Apple, R. W., Jr. "An Excess of the Pulpit, and Not Enough Bully." *New York Times*, August 5, 1993.

Arnold, Peri E. *Making the Managerial Presidency*. Princeton: Princeton University Press, 1986.

Asher, Herbert. *Presidential Elections and American Politics*. Homewood, Ill.: Dorsey Press, 1984.

Baker, Nancy V. *Conflicting Loyalties: Law and Politics in the Attorney General's Office, 1789–1990*. Lawrence: University Press of Kansas, 1992.

Barber, Benjamin R. "Neither Leaders nor Followers: Citizenship Under Strong Democracy." In *Essays in Honor of James MacGregor Burns*, edited by Thomas E. Cronin and Michael R. Beschloss. Englewood Cliffs, N.J.: Prentice-Hall, 1989.

———. *Strong Democracy: Participatory Politics for a New Age*. Berkeley: University of California Press, 1984.

Barber, James David. *Choosing the President*. New York: American Assembly, 1974.

———. "The Nixon Brush with Tyranny," *Political Science Quarterly* 92, no. 4 (winter 1977–78).

———. *The Presidential Character: Predicting Performance in the White House*. Englewood Cliffs, N.J.: Prentice-Hall, 1992.

Barger, Harold. *The Impossible Presidency: Illusions and Realities of Executive Power*. Glenview, Ill.: Scott, Foresman, 1984.

Barilleaux, Ryan J., and Barbara Kellerman. *The President as World Leader*. New York: St. Martin's Press, 1991.

Barnes, James A. "Ready or Not." *National Journal*, September 4, 1993.

Bell, Terrel. *The Thirteenth Man: A Reagan Cabinet Memoir*. New York: Free Press, 1987.

Bellah, Robert N., William Sullivan, Ann Swidel, and Steven Tipton. *Habits of the Heart*. New York: HarperCollins, 1985.

Bennis, Warren. *On Becoming a Leader*. Reading, Pa. Addison-Wesley, 1989.

———. *Why Leaders Can't Lead: The Unconscious Conspiracy Continues*. San Francisco: Jossey-Bass, 1989.

Bennis, Warren, and Burt Nanus. *Leaders: Strategies for Taking Charge*. New York: Harper-Collins, 1985.

Berman, Larry. *Lyndon Johnson's War*. New York: Norton, 1991.

———. *The New American Presidency*. Boston: Little, Brown, 1987.

Beschloss, Michael R., and Thomas E. Cronin. *Essays in Honor of James MacGregor Burns*. Englewood Cliffs, N.J.: Prentice-Hall, 1989.

Bessette, Joseph M., and Jeffrey Tulis. *The Presidency in the Constitutional Order*. Baton Rouge: Louisiana State University Press, 1984.

Blakesley, Lance. *The President as a Stratigically Versatile Leader*. Chicago: Nelson-Hall, 1995.

Blessing, Tim H., and Robert K. Murray. *Greatness in the White House: Rating the Presidents, Washington Through Carter*. University Park: Pennsylvania State University Press, 1988.

———. "The Presidential Performance Study: A Progress Report." *Journal of American History* 170 (1983).

Blumenthal, Sidney. "The Education of a President." *The New Yorker*, January 24, 1994.

Bond, Jon, and Richard Fleisher. *The President in the Legislative Arena*. Chicago: University of Chicago Press, 1990.

Brace, Paul, and Barbara Hinckley. *Follow the Leader: Opinion Polls and the Modern Presidents*. New York: Basic Books, 1992.

Breslin, Jimmy. *How the Good Guys Finally Won*. New York: Ballantine Books, 1975.

Brody, Richard A. *Assessing the President: The Media, Elite Opinion, and Public Support*. Stanford, Calif.: Stanford University Press, 1991.

Bryce, James. *The American Commonwealth*. New York: MacMillan, 1888.

Buchanan, Bruce. *The Presidential Experience: What the Office Does to the Man*. Englewood Cliffs, N.J.: Prentice-Hall, 1978.

Bunce, Valerie. *Do New Leaders Make a Difference?: Executive Successions and Public Policy Capitalism and Socialism*. Princeton: Princeton University Press, 1981.

Burke, John P. *The Institutional Presidency*. Baltimore: Johns Hopkins University Press, 1992.

Burns, James MacGregor. *Leadership*. New York: HarperCollins, 1978.

———. "More Than Merely Power: II." *New York Times*, November 17, 1978.

———. *The Power to Lead: The Crisis of the American Presidency*. New York: Simon & Schuster, 1984.

———. *Presidential Government: The Crucible of Leadership*. Boston: Houghton Mifflin, 1965.

———. *Roosevelt: The Lion and the Fox*. San Diego: Harvest/HBJ, 1984.

Campbell, Colin. *Managing the Presidency: Carter, Reagan, and the Search for Executive Harmony*. Pittsburgh: University of Pittsburgh Press, 1986.

———. "Political Executives and their Officials," *Political Science: The State of the Discipline, II*. Washington, D.C.: American Political Science Association, 1993.

Campbell, Colin, and Bert Rockman. *The Bush Presidency: First Appraisals*. Chatham, N.J.: Chatham House, 1991.

Cannon, Lou. *President Reagan: The Role of a Lifetime*. New York: Touchstone, 1991.

Cantrill, Albert. *The American People, Vietnam and the Presidency*. Princeton: Princeton University Press, 1976.

Ceasar, James W. *Presidential Selection*. Princeton: Princeton University Press, 1979.

Chubb, John E., and Paul E. Peterson. *Can the Government Govern?* Washington, D.C.: Brookings, 1989.

————. *The New Direction in American Politics*. Washington, D.C.: Brookings, 1985.

Clausen, Aage R. *How Congressmen Decide: A Policy Focus*. New York: St. Martin's Press, 1973.

Cohen, Jeffrey E. "A Historical Reassessment of Wildavsky's 'Two Presidencies' Thesis," *Social Science Quarterly* 63 (September 1982).

Corrado, Anthony. *Creative Campaigning*. Boulder, Colo.: Westview, 1992.

Corvitz, L. Gordon, and Jeremy A. Rabkin. *The Tethered Presidency*. Washington, D.C.: American Enterprise Institute, 1989.

Corwin, Edward S. *The President: Office and Powers, 1978–1984*. 5th ed. New York: New York University Press, 1984.

————. *Total War and the Constitution*. Westminster, Md.: Knopf, 1947.

Cotter, Cornelius P. and J. Malcolm Smith. *Powers of the President During Crises*. Washington, D.C.: Public Affairs Press, 1960.

Covington, Cary R., and Lester G. Seligman. *The Coalition Presidency*. Chicago: Dorsey Press, 1989.

Cox, Gary W., and Samuel Kernell. *The Politics of Divided Government*, Boulder, Colo.: Westview Press, 1991.

Crabb, Cecil V., and Kevin V. Mulcahy. *American National Security*. Pacific Grove, Calif.: Brookscole, 1991.

Cronin, Thomas E. "If Bush Is to Be the 'Education President' Much Work Must Be Done at the Grassroots." *Chronicle of Higher Education* 35, February 1, 1989.

————. *Inventing the American Presidency*. Lawrence: University Press of Kansas, 1989.

————. "Leadership and Democracy," *Liberal Education* 73, no. 2 (March/April 1987).

————. "Presidential Power Revised and Reappraised," *Western Political Quarterly*, December 1979.

————. *The State of the Presidency*. 2nd ed. Boston: Little, Brown, 1980.

————. "Superman, Our Textbook President," *The Washington Monthly*, October 1970.

————. "Thinking and Learning About Leadership," *Presidential Studies Quarterly*, winter 1984.

Cronin, Thomas E., and Michael R. Beschloss. *Essays in Honor of James MacGregor Burns*. Englewood Cliffs, N.J.: Prentice-Hall, 1989.

Crozier, Michael. *The Trouble with America*. Berkeley: University of California Press, 1984.

Cunliffe, Marcus. "A Defective Institution?" *Commentary*, February 1968.

Cutler, Lloyd. "Party Government Under the Constitution." In *Reforming American Government: The Bicentennial Papers of the Committee on the Constitutional System*. Boulder, Colo.: Westview Press, 1985.

Dahl, Robert A. *Pluralist Democracy in the United States*. New York: Rand McNally, 1967.

Davidson, Roger H. "The Presidency and Congress." In *The Presidency and the Political System*. Washington, D.C.: Congressional Quarterly Press, 1984.

Davis, James A., and David L. Nixon. "The President's Party." *Presidential Studies Quarterly* 24, no. 2 (spring 1994).

Davis, James W. *The American Presidency: A New Perspective*. New York: HarperCollins, 1987.

———. *The President as Party Leader*. New York: Praeger, 1992.

Deaver, Michael K. *Behind the Scenes*. New York: William Morrow, 1988.

DeGrazia, Alfred. *Congress and the Presidency*. Washington, D.C.: American Enterprise Institute, 1967.

———. *Republic in Crisis: Congress Against the Executive Force*. New York: Federal Legal Publications, 1965.

DiClerico, Robert E. *The American President*. Englewood Cliffs, N.J.: Prentice-Hall, 1979.

Draper, Theodore. *A Very Thin Line: The Iran-Contra Affairs*. New York: Touchstone Books, 1991.

Drucker, Peter. *The Effective Executive*. New York: HarperCollins, 1966.

Eastland, Terry. *Energy in the Executive*. New York: Free Press, 1992.

Edwards, George C. *At the Margins: Presidential Leadership in Congress*. New Haven: Yale University Press, 1989.

———. *The Public Presidency*. New York: St. Martin's Press, 1983.

Edwards, George C., John H. Kessel, and Bert A. Rockman. *Researching the Presidency: Vital Questions, New Approaches*. Pittsburgh: University of Pittsburgh Press, 1993.

Edwards, George C., and Stephen Wayne. *Presidential Leadership: Politics and Policy Making*. New York: St. Martin's Press, 1990.

Evans, Rowland, and Robert Novak. *Lyndon B. Johnson: The Exercise of Power*. New York: New American Library, 1966.

Fair, Ray C. "The Effect of Economic Events on Votes for President." *Review of Economics and Statistics* 60 (1978).

Ferrell, Robert H., ed. *Off the Record: The Private Papers of Harry S Truman*. New York: Harper-Collins, 1980.

Finer, Herman. *The Presidency*. Chicago: University of Chicago Press, 1960.

Finifter, Ada W. *Political Science: The State of the Discipline, III*. Washington, D.C.: American Political Science Association, 1993.

Fishel, Jeff. *Presidents and Promises*. Washington, D.C.: CQ Press, 1985.

Fisher, Louis. *The Constitution Between Friends*. New York: St. Martin's Press, 1978.

Fleisher, Richard, and Jon Bond. *The President in the Legislative Arena*. Chicago: University of Chicago Press, 1990.

Fortas, Abe. "The Constitution and the Presidency." *Washington Law Review* 49 (August 1974).

Franck, Thomas M. *Political Questions/Judicial Answers*. Princeton: Princeton University Press, 1992.

Franklin, Daniel P. *Extraordinary Measures*. Pittsburgh: University of Pittsburgh Press, 1991.

Gaebler, Ted, and David Osbourne. *Reinventing Government*. New York: Plume, 1992.

Gardner, John. *On Leadership*. New York: Free Press, 1990.

Genovese, Michael A. "Democratic Theory and the Emergency Powers of the President." *Presidential Studies Quarterly,* summer 1979.

————. *The Nixon Presidency: Power and Politics in Turbulent Times.* Westport, Conn.: Greenwood Press, 1990.

————. *The Presidency in an Age of Limits.* Westport, Conn.: Greenwood Press, 1993.

————"Presidents and Crisis: Developing a Crisis Management System in the Executive Branch." *International Journal on World Peace,* spring 1987.

————. "Presidential Leadership and Crisis Management." *Presidential Studies Quarterly,* spring 1986.

————. "The Return of the Imperial Presidency." *Presidency Research,* fall 1986.

————. *The Supreme Court, the Constitution, and the Presidential Power.* Lanham, Md.: University Press of America, 1980.

————. "The Supreme Court, as a Check on Presidential Power." *Presidential Studies Quarterly,* winter-spring 1976.

————. "Wimpyman, Our Textbook President." *Presidency Research,* winter 1988–89.

Genovese, Michael A., and Seth Thompson. "Women as Chief Executives: Does Gender Matter?" In *Women as National Leaders,* edited by Michael A. Genovese. Newbury Park, Calif.: Sage, 1993.

Gerstenzang, James, and Paul Richter. "Clinton Lobbying Wins More Votes for NAFTA Pact." *Los Angeles Times,* November 17, 1993, A1.

Ginsberg, Benjamin, and Martin Shefter. *Politics by Other Means.* New York: Basic Books, 1990.

Ginsberg, Benjamin, and Theodore J. Lowi. *Democrats Return to Power.* New York: Norton, 1994.

Golden, David G., and James M. Poterba. "The Price of Popularity: The Political Business Cycle Reexamined." *American Journal of Political Science* 24 (1980).

Greenberg, Edward. *The American Political System.* Boston: Little Brown, 1986.

Greenstein, Fred. "What the President Means to Americans." In *Choosing The President,* edited by James D. Barber. New York: American Assembly, 1974.

————. *The Hidden-Hand Presidency: Eisenhower as Leader.* New York: Basic Books, 1982.

Greenstein, Fred I., and Nelson Polsby. *The Handbook of Political Theory: Micro-Political Theory.* Reading, Pa.: Addison-Wesley, 1975.

Grossman, Michael Baruch, and Martha Joynt Kumar. "Carter, Reagan and the Media: Have the Rules Changed or the Poles of the Spectrum of Success?" Paper presented at the annual meeting of the American Political Science Association, New York, September 1981.

Grover, William F. *The President as Prisoner.* New York: State University of New York Press, 1989.

Haig, Alexander M. *Caveat: Realism, Reagan and Foreign Policy.* New York: Macmillan, 1984.

Halberstan, David. *The Best and the Brightest.* New York: Random House, 1972.

Hamilton, Alexander, James Madison, and John Jay. *Federalist Papers.* New York: New American Library, 1961.

Hargrove, Erwin C. *Jimmy Carter as President: A Study of Policy Leadership.* Baton Rouge: Louisiana State University Press, 1988.

————. *The Power of the Modern Presidency*. New York: Knopf, 1974.

————. "Presidential Personality and Leadership Style." In *Researching the Presidency: Vital Questions, New Approaches*. Pittsburgh: University of Pittsburgh Press, 1993.

Harriger, Katy J. *Independent Justice: The Federal Special Prosecutor in American Politics*. Lawrence: University Press of Kansas, 1992.

Hart, Roderick. *The Sound of Leadership* Chicago: University of Chicago Press, 1987.

Heclo, Hugh. *A Government of Strangers: Executive Politics in Washington*. Washington, D.C.: Brookings, 1977.

Heclo, Hugh, and Lester Salamon. *The Illusion of Presidential Government*. Boulder, Colo.: Westview Press, 1981.

Hertsgaard, Mark. *On Bended Knee: The Press and the Reagan Presidency*. New York: Schocken Books, 1989.

Hess, Stephen. *Organizing the Presidency*. Washington, D.C.: Brookings, 1977.

Hinckley, Barbara, and Paul Brace. *Follow the Leader: Opinion Polls and the Modern Presidents*. New York: Basic Books, 1992.

Hodgson, Godfrey. *All Things to All Men*. New York: Touchstone, 1980.

Hofstadter, Richard. *The Idea of a Party System*. Oxford: Oxford University Press, 1969.

Hughes, Emmet John. *The Living Presidency*. New York: Coward, McCann and Geoghegan, 1973.

Huntington, Samuel P. *American Politics: The Promise of Disharmony*. Cambridge: Harvard University Press, 1981.

Jehl, Douglas. "Clinton Assails G.O.P. Delays in Bitter Tones." *New York Times*, July 27, 1993.

Johnson, Richard T. *Managing the White House*. New York: HarperCollins, 1974.

Jones, Charles O. *The Presidency in a Separated System*. Washington, D.C.: Brookings, 1994.

Kann, Mark E. "Challenging Lockean Liberalism in America: The Case of Debs and Hillquit." *Political Theory*, no. 8 (May 1980).

Karnow, Stanley. *Vietnam: A History*. New York: Viking, 1983.

Kellerman, Barbara, and Ryan J. Barilleaux. *The President as World Leader*. New York: St. Martin's Press, 1991.

Kennedy, John F. Foreword to Theodore C. Sorenson, *Decision-Making in the White House*. New York: Columbia University Press, 1963.

Kennedy, Paul. *The Rise and Fall of the Great Powers*. New York: Vintage Books, 1987.

Kernell, Samuel M. "Explaining Presidential Popularity." *American Political Science Review* 72 (1978).

————. *Going Public: New Strategies of Presidential Leadership*. Washington, D.C.: Congressional Quarterly Press, 1986.

Kernell, Samuel, and Gary W. Cox. *The Politics of Divided Government*. Boulder, Colo.: Westview Press, 1991.

Kernell, Samuel, and Samuel Popkin, eds. *Chief of Staff*. Berkeley: University of California Press, 1986.

Kessel, John H. *Presidential Campaign Politics*. Chicago: Dorsey Press, 1988.

Kessel, John H., George C. Edwards, and Bert A. Rockman. *Researching the Presidency: Vital Questions, New Approaches.* Pittsburgh: University of Pittsburgh Press, 1993.

King, Gary, and Lyn Ragsdale. *The Elusive Executive.* Washington, D.C.: CQ Press, 1988.

Koenig, Louis W. *The Chief Executive.* San Diego: Harcourt Brace Jovanovich, 1980.

Koh, Harold Kongju. *The National Security Constitution: Sharing Power After the Iran-Contra Affair.* New Haven: Yale University Press, 1990.

Kozak, David C. "Some Thoughts on Clinton's Challengers." *Presidential Studies Quarterly,* fall 1993.

Kraft, Joseph. "The Post Imperial Presidency." *The New York Times,* November 1, 1980.

Kumar, Martha Joynt, and Michael Baruch Grossman. "Carter, Reagan, and the Media: Have the Rules Changed or the Poles of the Spectrum of Success?" Paper presented at the annual meeting of the American Political Science Association. New York, September 1981.

Kutler, Stanley, K. *The Wars of Watergate.* New York: Knopf, 1990.

Lammers, William W. *Presidential Politics: Patterns and Prospects.* New York: HarperCollins, 1976.

LeLoup, Lance T., and Steven A. Shull. *Congress and the President: The Policy Connection.* Belmont: Wadsworth, 1993.

———. "Congress Versus the Executive: The 'Two Presidencies' Reconsidered." *Social Science Quarterly* 59 (March 1979).

Lerner, Max. *America as a Civilization.* New York: Knopf, 1957.

Leuchtenburg, William E. *In the Shadow of FDR: From Harry Truman to Ronald Reagan.* Ithaca, N.Y.: Cornell University Press, 1983.

Lifton, Robert Jay. *The Protean Self: Resilence In an Age of Fragmentation.* New York: Basic Books, 1993.

Light, Paul C. *The President's Agenda.* Baltimore: Johns Hopkins University Press, 1982.

Lindblom, Charles E. "The Market as Prison." *The Journal of Politics* 44 (1982).

Lindsay, James M., and Wayne P. Steger. "The Two Presidencies in Future Research: Moving Beyond Roll-Call Analysis." *Congress and the Presidency* 20, no. 2 (autumn 1993).

Locke, John. *Treatise on Civil Government and a Letter Concerning Toleration.* New York: Appleton-Century-Crofts, 1937.

Longaker, Richard, ed. Clinton Rossiter, *The Supreme Court and the Commander in Chief,* expanded ed. (Ithaca, N.Y.: Cornell University Press, 1976).

Lowi, Theodore J. *The Personal President: Power Invested Promise Unfulfilled.* Ithaca, N.Y.: Cornell University Press, 1985.

Lowi, Theodore J., and Benjamin Ginsberg. *Democrats Return to Power.* New York: Norton, 1994.

Machiavelli, Niccolò. *The Prince and the Discourses.* New York: Modern Library, 1950.

Mansfield, Harvey C. Jr. *Taming the Prince.* New York: The Free Press, 1989.

Mattise, John. *Spin Control: The White House Office and Communications and the Management of Presidential News.* Chapel Hill: University of North Carolina Press, 1992.

Mayer, Jane, and Doyle McManus. *Landslide: The Unmaking of the President, 1984–1988.* Boston: Houghton Mifflin, 1988.

Mayhew, David. *Congress: The Electoral Connection*. New Haven: Yale University Press, 1974.

———. *Divided We Govern*. New Haven: Yale University Press, 1991.

McConnell, Grant. *The Modern Presidency*. New York: St. Martin's Press, 1967.

Meyers, Frank E. "Social Classes and Political Change in Western Industrial Systems." *Comparative Politics* 2 (1970).

Milkis, Sidney M. *The President and the Parties*. New York: Oxford University Press, 1993.

Mill, John Stuart. *Considerations on Representative Government*. New York: Liberal Arts Press, 1958.

Miroff, Bruce. *Icons of Democracy*. New York: Basic Books, 1993.

———. *Pragmatic Illusions*. New York: David McKay, 1976.

Moe, Terry M. "The Politicized Presidency." In *The New Direction in American Politics*. Washington, D.C.: Brookings, 1985.

———. "Presidential Style and Presidential Theory." Paper presented at the Presidency Research Conference, Pittsburgh, November 1990.

Moore, Raymond A., Marcia Lynn Whicker, and James P. Pfiffner. *The Presidency and the Persian Gulf War*. Westport, Conn.: Praeger, 1993.

Mosley, Zelma, Joseph Pika, and Richard A. Watson. *The Presidential Contest*. Washington, D.C.: CQ Press, 1992.

Murray, Robert K., and Tim H. Blessing. *Greatness in the White House: Rating the Presidents, Washington Through Carter*. University Park: Pennsylvania State University Press, 1988.

———. "The Presidential Performance Study: A Progress Report." *Journal of American History* 170 (1983).

Nanus, Bert. *Visionary Leadership*. San Francisco: Jossey-Bass, 1992.

Nanus, Bert, and Warren Bennis. *Leaders: The Strategies for Taking Charge*. New York: HarperCollins, 1985.

Nathan, Richard. *The Administrative Presidency*. New York: Wiley, 1983.

Nelson, Michael. "Evaluating the Presidency." In *The Presidency and the Political System*. Washington, D.C.: CQ Press, 1984.

Neustadt, Richard E. *Presidential Power*. New York: Wiley, 1960.

———. *Presidential Power and the Modern Presidents*. New York: Free Press, 1990.

———. *Presidential Power: The Politics of Leadership*. New York: Wiley, 1976.

Nixon, David L., and James A. Davis. "The President's Party." *Presidential Studies Quarterly* 24, no. 2 (spring 1994).

Novak, Robert, and Rowland Evans. *Lyndon B. Johnson: The Exercise of Power*. New York: New American Library, 1966.

Novak, William, and Thomas P. O'Neill. *Man of the House: The Life and Political Memoirs of Speaker Tip O'Neill*. New York: Random House, 1987.

Nye, Joseph. *Bound to Lead*. New York: Basic Books, 1990.

O'Connor, James. *The Fiscal Crisis of the State*. New York: St. Martin's Press, 1973.

O'Neill, Thomas P., with William Novak. *Man of the House: The Life and Political Memoirs of Speaker Tip O'Neill*. New York: Random House, 1987.

Oldfield, Duane M., and Aaron Wildavsky. "Reconsidering the Two Presidencies." *Society*, July/August 1989.

Orman, John. "Covering the American Presidency: Valanced Reporting in the Presidential Press." *Presidential Studies Quarterly* 14 (1984).

Ornstein, Norman, and Michael Robinson. "The Case of Our Disappearing Congress." *TV Guide*, January 11, 1986.

Peterson, Merrill D., ed. *The Portable Thomas Jefferson*. New York: Viking Press, 1975.

Peterson, Paul, and John Chubb. *Can the Government Govern?* Washington, D.C.: Brookings, 1989.

————. *The New Direction in American Politics*. Washington, D.C.: Brookings, 1985.

Pfiffner, James P. "The Carter-Reagan Transition: Hitting the Ground Running." *Presidential Studies Quarterly*, fall 1983.

————. ed. *The Managerial Presidency*. Pacific Grove, Calif.: Brooks/Cove, 1991.

————. *The Modern Presidency*. New York: St. Martin's Press, 1993.

————. "The President's Chief of Staff: Lessons Learned." Working Paper 92:19, October 1992, *The Institute of Public Policy*. George Mason University.

————. *The Strategic Presidency: Hitting the Ground Running*. Chicago: Dorsey Press, 1988.

Pfiffner, James P., Marcia Lynn Whicker, and Raymond A. Moore. *The Presidency and the Persian Gulf War*. Westport, Conn.: Praeger, 1993.

Phelps, Glen A. *George Washington and American Constitutionalism*. Lawrence: University Press of Kansas, 1993.

Phillips, Donald T. *Lincoln on Leadership*. New York: Warner Books, 1992.

Pika, Joseph A., Zelma Mosley, and Richard A. Watson. *The Presidential Contest*. Washington D.C.: CQ Press, 1992.

Pika, Joseph A., Norman C. Thomas, and Richard A. Watson. *The Politics of the Presidency* Washington, D.C.: CQ Press, 1993.

Pious, Richard M. *The American Presidency*. New York: Basic Books, 1979.

Polsby, Nelson, and Fred I. Greenstein. *The Handbook of Political Theory: Micro-Political Theory*. Reading, Pa.: Addison-Wesley, 1975.

Polsby, Nelson W., and Aaron Wildavsky. *Presidential Elections*. New York: Free Press, 1991.

Popkin, Samuel, and Samuel Kernell. *Chief of State*. Berkeley: University of California Press, 1986.

Porter, Roger. "Gerald Ford: A Healing Presidency." In *Leadership in the Modern Presidency*, edited by Fred I. Greenstein. Cambridge: Harvard University Press, 1988.

Poterba, James M., and David G. Golden. "The Price of Popularity: The Political Business Cycle Reexamined." *American Journal of Political Science* 24 (1980).

Rabkin, Jeremy A., and L. Gordon Corvitz. *The Tethered Presidency*. Washington, D.C.: American Enterprise Institute, 1989.

Ragsdale, Lyn. *Presidential Politics*. Boston: Houghton Mifflin, 1993.

Ragsdale, Lyn, and Gary King. *The Elusive Executive*. Washington, D.C.: CQ Press, 1988.

Randall, Willard Sterne. *Thomas Jefferson: A Life*. New York: Henry Holt, 1993.

Richter, Paul, and James Gerstenzang. "Clinton Lobbying Wins More Votes for NAFTA Pact." *Los Angeles Times*, November 17, 1993.

Richter, Paul, and Karen Tamulty. "Clinton's Use of the Soft Sell Worries Allies." *Los Angeles Times*, July 31, 1993.

Rimmerman, Craig A. *Presidency by Plebiscite*. Boulder, Colo.: Westview Press, 1993.

Rivers, Douglas, and Nancy Rose. "Passing the President's Program: Public Opinion and Presidential Influence in Congress." *American Journal of Political Science* 29 (May 1985).

Robinson, Donald L. *"To the Best of My Ability": The Presidency and the Constitution*. New York: Norton, 1987.

Robinson, Michael, and Norman Ornstein. "The Case of Our Disappearing Congress." *TV Guide*, January, 11, 1986.

Robinson, Michael J., and Margaret A. Sheehan. *Over the Wire and on TV*. New York: Russell Sage Foundation, 1983.

Rockman, Bert. *The Leadership Question: The Presidency and the American System*. New York: Praeger, 1984.

Rockman, Bert, and Colin Campbell. *The Bush Presidency: First Appraisals*. Chatham, N.J.: Chatham House, 1991.

Rockman, Bert A., George C. Edwards, and John H. Kessel. *Researching the Presidency: Vital Questions, New Approaches*. Pittsburgh: University of Pittsburgh Press, 1993.

Rose, Nancy, and Douglas Rivers. "Passing the President's Program: Public Opinion and Presidential Influence in Congress." *American Journal of Political Science* 29 (May 1985).

Rose, Richard. *The Postmodern President: The White House Meets the World*. Chatham, N.J.: Chatham House, 1991.

Rossiter, Clinton. *The American Presidency*. New York: Harcourt, Brace and World, 1956.

———. *Conservatism in America*. New York: Vintage, 1962.

———. *Constitutional Dictatorship: Crisis Government in the Modern Democracy*. Princeton: Princeton University Press, 1948.

Rousseau, Jean Jacques. *Social Contract*. New York: Dutton, 1950.

Sabato, Larry. *Feeding Frenzy*. New York: Free Press, 1991.

Salamon, Lester, and Hugh Heclo. *The Illusion of Presidential Government*. Boulder, Colo.: Westview Press, 1981.

Salokar, Rebecca Mae. *The Solicitor General*. Philadelphia: Temple University Press, 1992.

Schlesinger, Arthur M., Jr. *The Cycles of American History*. Boston: Houghton Mifflin, 1986.

———. *The Imperial Presidency*. Boston: Houghton Mifflin, 1973.

———. "Leave the Constitution Alone," in Donald Robinson, ed., *Reforming American Government: The Bicentennial Papers of the Committee on the Constitutional System*. Boulder, Colo.: Westview Press, 1985.

———. *A Thousand Days: John F. Kennedy in the White House*. Boston: Houghton Mifflin, 1965.

Schlesinger, Arthur M., Jr., and Alfred de Grazia. *Congress and the Presidency: Their Role in Modern Times*. Washington, D.C.: American Enterprise Institute, 1967.

Schubert, Glendon. *The Presidency in the Courts*. Minneapolis: University of Minnesota Press, 1957.

Shuman, David F. *A Preface to Politics*. Hasca, Ill.: F. E. Peacock, 1991.

Seligman, Lester G., and Cary R. Covington. *The Coalition Presidency*. Chicago: Dorsey Press, 1989.

Shaw, David. "Covering Clinton: Did Media Rush to Judgment or Merely Reflect Reality?" *Los Angeles Times*, September 15, 16, 17, 1993.

Sheehan, Margaret A., and Michael J. Robinson. *Over the Wire and on TV.* New York: Russell Sage Foundation, 1983.

Shefter, Martin, and Benjamin Ginsberg. *Politics by Other Means.* New York: Basic Books, 1990.

Shogan, Robert. *The Riddle of Power.* New York: Dutton, 1991.

Shull, Steven A., ed. *The Two Presidencies: A Quarter Century Assessment.* Chicago: Nelson-Hall, 1991.

Shull, Steven A., and Lance T. LeLoup. "Congress Versus the Executive: The Two Presidencies Reconsidered." *Social Science Quarterly* 59 (March 1979).

————. *Congress and President: The Policy Connection.* Belmont: Wadsworth, 1993.

Sigelman, Lee. "A Reassessment of the Two Presidencies' Thesis." *Journal of Politics* 41 (November 1979).

Skowronek, Stephen. *The Politics Presidents Make.* Cambridge, Mass.: Belknap, 1993.

————. "Presidential Leadership in Political Times." In *The President and the Political System,* edited by Michael J. Nelson. 3rd ed. Washington, D.C.: CQ Press, 1990.

Smith, Hedrick. *The Power Game: How Washington Works.* New York: Ballantine, 1988.

Smith, J. Malcolm, and Cornelius P. Cotter. *Powers of the President During Crises.* Washington, D.C.: Public Affairs Press, 1960.

Sorensen, Theodore C. *Watchmen in the Night.* Cambridge: MIT Press, 1975.

Speakes, Larry. *Speaking Out.* New York: Scribners, 1988.

Spitzer, Robert J. *President and Congress: Executive Hegemony at the Crossroads of American Government.* New York: McGraw-Hill, 1993.

————. *The Presidential Veto: Touchstone of the American Presidency.* Albany: State University of New York Press, 1988.

Stegar, Wayne P., and James M. Lindsay. "The Two Presidencies in Future Research: Moving Beyond Roll-Call Analysis." *Congress and the Presidency* 20, no. 2 (autumn 1993).

Stockman, David A. *The Triumph of Politics: The Inside Story of the Reagan Revolution.* New York: Avon, 1987.

Stuckey, Mary E. *The President as Interpreter-in-Chief.* Chatham, N.J.: Chatham House, 1991.

Sullivan, Terry. "Headcounts, Expectations and Presidential Coalitions in Congress." *American Journal of Political Science* 32:3 (August 1988).

Sundquist, James L. *Constitutional Reform and Effective Government.* Washington, D.C.: Brookings, 1986.

Sundquist, James L. "Needed: A Political Theory for the New Era of Coalition Government in the United States." *Political Science Quarterly* 103, winter 1988.

Tamulty, Karen. "Clinton Piles Up Record Legislative Wins." *Los Angeles Times,* November 13, 1993, A23.

Tamulty, Karen, and Paul Richter. "Clinton's Use of the Soft Sell Worries Allies." *Los Angeles Times,* July 31, 1993.

Thompson, Seth, and Michael A. Genovese. "Women as Chief Executives: Does Gender Matter?" In *Women as National Leaders,* edited by Michael A. Genovese. Newbury Park, Calif.: Sage, 1993.

Thurber, James A. *Divided Democracy.* Washington, D.C.: CQ Press, 1991.

Tocqueville, Alexis de. *Democracy in America.* New York: Knopf, 1969.

Tulis, Jeffrey K. *The Rhetorical Presidency.* Princeton: Princeton University Press, 1987.

Tulis, Jeffrey, and Joseph Bessette. *The Presidency in the Constitutional Order.* Baton Rouge: Louisiana State University, 1981.

Watson, Richard A. *The Presidential Contest.* New York: Wiley, 1984.

Watson, Richard A., Norman C. Thomas, and Joseph A. Pika. *The Politics of the Presidency.* Washington, D.C.: CQ Press, 1993.

Wayne, Stephen J. *The Road to the White House.* New York: St. Martin's Press, 1988.

Wayne, Stephen J., and George Edwards. *Presidential Leadership: Politics and Policy Making.* New York: St. Martin's Press, 1990.

Whicker, Marcia Lynn, James P. Pfiffner, and Raymond A. Moore, eds. *The Presidency and the Persian Gulf War.* Westport, Conn.: Praeger, 1993.

Wildavsky, Aaron. "The Two Presidencies." In *Perspectives on the Presidency.* Boston: Little, Brown, 1975.

Wildavsky, Aaron, and Duane M. Oldfield. "Reconsidering the Two Presidencies." *Society,* July/August 1989.

Will, George. "The Veep and the Blatherskite." *Newsweek,* June 29, 1992.

Williams, Phil. "The Limits of American Power: From Nixon to Reagan." *International Affairs,* autumn 1987.

Williams, Walter. *Mismanaging America: The Rise of the Anti-Analytic Presidency.* Lawrence: University Press of Kansas, 1990.

Wilson, Woodrow. *The State.* Boston: D. C. Heath, 1903.

Wolfe, Alan. *The Limits of Legitimacy.* New York: Free Press, 1977.

Wolin, Sheldon. *Politics and Vision.* Boston: Little, Brown, 1960.

Young, James S. *The Washington Community, 1800–1828.* New York: Columbia University Press, 1966.

Zeidenstein, Harvey G. "Presidents' Popularity and Their Wins and Losses on Major Issues: Does One Have a Greater Influence over the Other?" *Presidential Studies Quarterly,* spring 1985.

INDEX